## Praise for *Mom's in There*

"*Mom's in There* is brilliant. Devastating, funny, and full of truth."
— Michael Goldfarb, journalist, author, and host of *FRDH, First Rough Draft of History* podcast

"*Mom's in There* gives us an intimate lens into the back and forth of a slow traveling and unraveling, the rises and falls, the good, the bad, and the terrible. This dramatic narrative is compelling in the intensity of its psychological self-examination."
— Merrill Leffler, publisher at Dryad Press, and author of the poetry collection, *Mark the Music*

"*Mom's in There* is a testament to the often overlooked and remarkable creative power of being with. Readers are offered rich glimpses into the private space of a woman dying, with her daughter at her side. The universal letting go is narrated most often by the ever-present daughter, sketchbook in hand, recording this poignant passage from life to death with attentive language and evocative drawings."
— Marianne Maili, author of *Lucy, go see.* and *I am home*

"*Mom's in There* captured me; I read every word. I liked the sparse but exacting details and the honest voice. I loved the illustrations."
— Romy Nordlinger, Actor/Screenwriter/Audiobook Narrator

"*Mom's in There* is a very moving book. There's little that's unique in the story itself—a woman slowly dies while her daughter and a bunch of strangers care for her. It's modern American death 101. But the telling is unique, and the art takes it beyond simple uniqueness to rare heights of the intensely personal."
— Daniel Kempner, journalist and author of the forthcoming book, *Saigon Serenade*

"*Mom's in There* is a nudge to perception. I was moved by the particular, pure voice of dying it expresses."
— Jacquie Morris, caregiver

"*Mom's in There* is genuine, real, and at the same time, sad and beautiful. Life and death meet and coexist in their full rawness and beauty. I hear it, feel it, and sense it, and it brings alive what I have experienced with my parents."
— Mari Rantamaki, MD

"I ended *Mom's in There* with an aching heart. Sorrow, yes, yet a sorrow that comes after reading a beautiful poem, a strange mix of beauty and truth combined that sneaks around your brain and settles into your heart. The paintings and pictures are powerful in context; the art speaks of moments of simple beauty and truth. They also powerfully invite me, as a reader, to a time of rest and reflection before going back into the room."
— Pastor Ed Koffenberger

"This simple, almost childlike, book is a doorway to wonder! With little commentary or interpretation, the author records her mother's words and the scenes through her window during the last months of her life. Without sensing the author as an intermediary, I felt that I was there in person, joining her mother as she made the journey from anxiety to wonder, and from prose to poetry. This sweet story soothed my own fears of dying and brought glimpses of the Great Life beyond."

—Swami Divyananda Ma, Integral Yoga

"I was awed by the portrayal of this deeply personal and intimate journey to death. At parts, I laughed out loud, at other parts, I felt a deep ache. Throughout, I felt profound compassion for this dying woman finding her way out."

—Ellah Ray, midwife

"It's troubling. Beautiful. Sad and joyous. One of the best pieces I've ever read about dying—both the experience of the dying, and those they are leaving."

—Damon Silvers, attorney, Visiting Professor of Practice, University College London

"*Mom's in There* is intimate, matter-of-fact, and kind. I was riveted and amazed. The paintings are incredible and help set the place. This book should be made accessible to anyone encountering an intimate death because it makes the end of life feel so miraculous."

—Matt Chapman, public school teacher

"*Mom's in There* is perfectly crafted, a work to be savored."

—Fred Liss, teacher of English as a Second Language.

"The author has given us a portrait of one person's dying. It has depth and strength without being 'sappy.' *Mom's in There* is so intimate that it's not a book, it's an experience."

—Jerry Carpenter, Mom's husband

"This is Mom's story—brave, troubled, funny, smart, rhyming and singing her way to her next life. The writing is unique: spare, direct, no egoism, honest. The lovely artwork is intriguing, comforting, and uplifting."

—Joy Payne, Mom's neighbor and walking companion

"The illustrations provide a sense of place. This in-depth reflection will provide another resource for a hospice team."

—Arlene FitzGerald, Mom's lifelong childhood friend

# Mom's in There

# Mom's in There

## KIRANA STOVER

Brandylane Publishers, Inc.
*Publishing books since 1985*

Copyright © 2026 by Kirana Stover

All rights reserved. No part of this book may be reproduced in any form or by any electronic or mechanical means, or the facilitation thereof, including information storage and retrieval systems, without permission in writing from the publisher, except in the case of brief quotations published in articles and reviews. Any educational institution wishing to photocopy part or all of the work for classroom use, or individual researchers who would like to obtain permission to reprint the work for educational purposes, should contact the publisher.

ISBN (Paperback): 978-1-966369-45-5
ISBN (Hardcover): 978-1-966369-44-8
ISBN (eBook): 978-1-966369-46-2
Library of Congress Control Number: 2025915653

Designed by Sami Langston
Project managed by Liz Knapp

Published by
Brandylane Publishers, Inc.
5 S. 1st Street
Richmond, Virginia 23219

brandylanepublishers.com

To Fred, whose mom had still so much to do.

"Live with me; stay here," Mom repeats.

"Are you saying you want me to move in with you and hang out with you all the time?"

"Yes."

"Jesus, Mom."

*I am home.*
Marianne Maili.

I have never seen
Spring unfold in quite this way.
Flowers bloom and fade.
(haiku, 28 March, 2023)

On Thursday, January 26, 2023, the landline phone rings. I know it will be my mom, calling to sing me happy birthday. I listen as she begins the familiar tune; this time the words turn out to be a little different.

*"Happy birthday to you*
*Happy birthday to us*
*We did it together,*
*Without too much fuss."*

"*I remember when I went into labor with you and took the bus downtown,*" she says.

That's the first time I realize she went to the hospital on her own to give birth to me.

After the song, I know something is wrong.

I visited my mom and her husband in the Spring of 2022 when almost all the lockdown restrictions had finally been lifted. Both in their eighties, they contracted Covid-19, the "breakthrough" Delta variant, in August 2021. They never got out of the house to be tested, but their doctor confirmed by phone that the symptoms they described were most likely Covid-19. They got better but never returned to their previous baseline wellness. They self-diagnosed long Covid.

In May of 2022, my mom had a light, lingering cough and got out of breath while walking quickly to keep up with my wheelchair assistance when she met me at the airport.

We went to an exhibit at the Virginia Museum of Fine Arts. It was about American painters who had been influenced by Impressionism. They had gone to France and come back. We had a wonderful lunch there, on a balcony that overlooked a sculpture of a twenty-four-foot white marble face.

*"I feel I can pretty much allow myself anything now,"* she told me.

We drove down Monument Avenue, empty now of monuments, just an avenue with monumental trees and houses.

I was still recovering from a head injury; sometimes she had more stamina than I did. She continued to get out of breath now and then, but overall, she had energy. The long Covid theory made some sense.

We went for walks around the Bellevue area. She showed me the ravine behind her cousin's childhood home. Despite having grown up there and walked that area countless times myself, I had never been in that enchanted ravine. Lightning Bug Alley, some people called it. It was like a tiny visit to Narnia with my mom.

We sat on the bench of the new stone-paved area recently built across from her house. She called it *"the patio."*

## 26 January

I know from the May visit that things are not easy for them. Her husband is almost housebound due to a stroke some years earlier. She has been walking outside less and walking with a cane inside the house since slipping in November.

After the birthday song, my mind begins to wonder about their long Covid theory. I recall my friend Ursula, whose cancer moved to her lungs. I realize my mom's cough last May sounded like Ursula's.

That weekend, I go to Palamós, on the Catalan coast, for a birthday getaway with my partner of fourteen years. My son is in Berlin as part of his university program and will be away until the end of February; this is a new phase of my life. Over dinner at the Hotel Trias, it dawns on me that I could visit my mom and her husband – just for two weeks – to check in and see how they are faring.

I call on Sunday when we arrive home. My mom's husband answers the telephone.

"I'm thinking of coming for two weeks to help out," I tell him.

"Oh, that would be wonderful!" He's rarely enthusiastic about visitors; this must be serious.

He passes the phone to my mom. In a resigned voice she says, *"I don't know how you could help."*

I explain various ways I could help. She's not convinced. *"It means so much to know that you want to come, that you care enough."*

"Well, what do you say, Mom, shall I come, or not?"

*"I'm just flummoxed."*

I decide to go.

Monday morning, my mom can't get out of bed to get to the bathroom. An ambulance comes and takes her to the hospital. She is diagnosed with metastasized breast cancer. It has gone to her spine, her lungs, and her uterus. There are three tumors in her brain. There is nothing to be done.

*"Do I have a month?"* My mom asks the doctor.

"Yes," the doctor replies.

*Sitges Cemetery*

Home hospice care is impossible, the house is too crowded, and her husband would be overwhelmed. She isn't dying soon enough to qualify for hospice care at the hospital. Because she is continent, feeding herself, and able to "stand and pivot," she qualifies for assisted living. My stepsister and my sister-in-law find an assisted living community that accepts her. She will be a resident with external hospice care. The three of us meet the administration on a Zoom call. My sister-in-law mentions that I will be coming to visit from Spain and asks if it is possible for me to stay there for a few nights with my mom. There are two rooms; they will order a sofa bed. For now, there is a twin bed. After our call, the assisted living community has an idea for a pilot project: this will become a hospice suite, and families will be allowed to stay with their loved ones during their last weeks of life. I will be the first! It will take a few days to get the paperwork done. Meanwhile, my mom is moved from the hospital to a skilled nursing home.

I book my ticket for February 6th. While still in Spain, I speak to my mother by phone. *"I guess you've been the best daughter you knew how to be."*

Should I respond in kind – "I guess you've been the best mother you knew how to be."?

*"I am proud of you for being strong for yourself when there was no one to be strong for you,"* she tells me.

## 6 February

Into the depths.

On the flight from Barcelona to JFK.

Last stop: Richmond.

Last year, I told my brother it was a beautiful and interesting city. "Take a vacation," I said, "Show your family where you grew up. See how it's changed. Visit them briefly. Take day trips with our mother." He didn't want to. Didn't see the point.

Now she's dying. Our mother. That expression "riddled with cancer" takes on meaning. It's in her spine, in her brain, a collapsed lung.

Now, less than two weeks since my fifty-eighth birthday, my mom is in the hospital, dying. I am on a flight from Barcelona to JFK – last stop: Richmond. My brother is coming next weekend with my sister-in-law.

Ten years ago, after a divorce, my best friend from high school moved back to the neighborhood we grew up in. At midnight, I take a taxi from the airport to her house.

The next morning, I walk to my mom's – the house we moved into when I was nine – and have breakfast with her husband: raisin bread toast with peanut butter. He hasn't seen his wife since she went to the hospital a week ago.

I go to the nursing home. The syntax of my mom's language has changed. She speaks in the present tense or even drops verbs.

*"I love you,"* she says, *"you good daughter." "Martha good sister."* She is telling all kinds of things.

After a long foray describing how people just do what they want, she sums it all up in a noun-only sentence: *"People, people."*

My mom is writing her obituary for the *Richmond Times Dispatch*.

*"I saw my diagnosis,"* she tells everybody, *"I know I got to let my soul go free."*

*"My Daddy told me,"* she says, *"Everybody gotta die."*

## 8 February

My mom is talking to my brother on the phone. She seems better today. She's had a shower, and her hair is washed. Who knows? Maybe she'll be here more than a month.

    With my stepsister, I visit the assisted living community in person. My mom will be moved there tomorrow. It's wonderful. Kind women run it. We will stay in the suite; there is a common area, and my room is adjacent to hers. When I was born, we did something called "Rooming-in," now we will do it in reverse!

## 9 February

I follow the transport car to the assisted living community. It's much better than the nursing home, but my mom is complaining. Transitions are difficult!

Then, in the night, she sees the moon rise through the window and behind Winter trees. She calls me to see it. *"The moon has come!"*

Title: *"Waning Moon My Tree South. Louna visited me there."*

My mom draws the moon rising in a journal I found in the offices of the assisted living community. She colors it the next morning with the crayons I brought.

We meet the hospice nurse. She tells me that a change in language syntax can be a sign of the end nearing.

My brother and sister-in-law arrive from California. They haven't seen our mother in person in eleven years. My mom's husband also comes to visit. In her journal, my mom writes, *"We party! We get to share stories old and new."* We all sit in the little kitchen area, my mom in her wheelchair.

Of the meeting with her husband she writes, *"We eyes light up. We kiss. He touched my hands and back and knows I'm 'Still Here.'"*

*"He need me,"* she tells me, *"but he just have to let go. Like me."*

One of her complaints about the assisted living community is that there is no clock in the room. Clocks are essential. My sister-in-law orders a clock. It shows the time, the date, the day of the week, and "morning," "afternoon," "evening," "night", "after midnight," (she discovers that one when she wakes at 2:45 a.m. to have Ensure and Lorna Doones) and "before dawn." She names it *"Clockey,"* then changes her mind and settles on *"Master Clock."* She declares it will go to her husband when she is gone. Now she knows where she is in time and space.

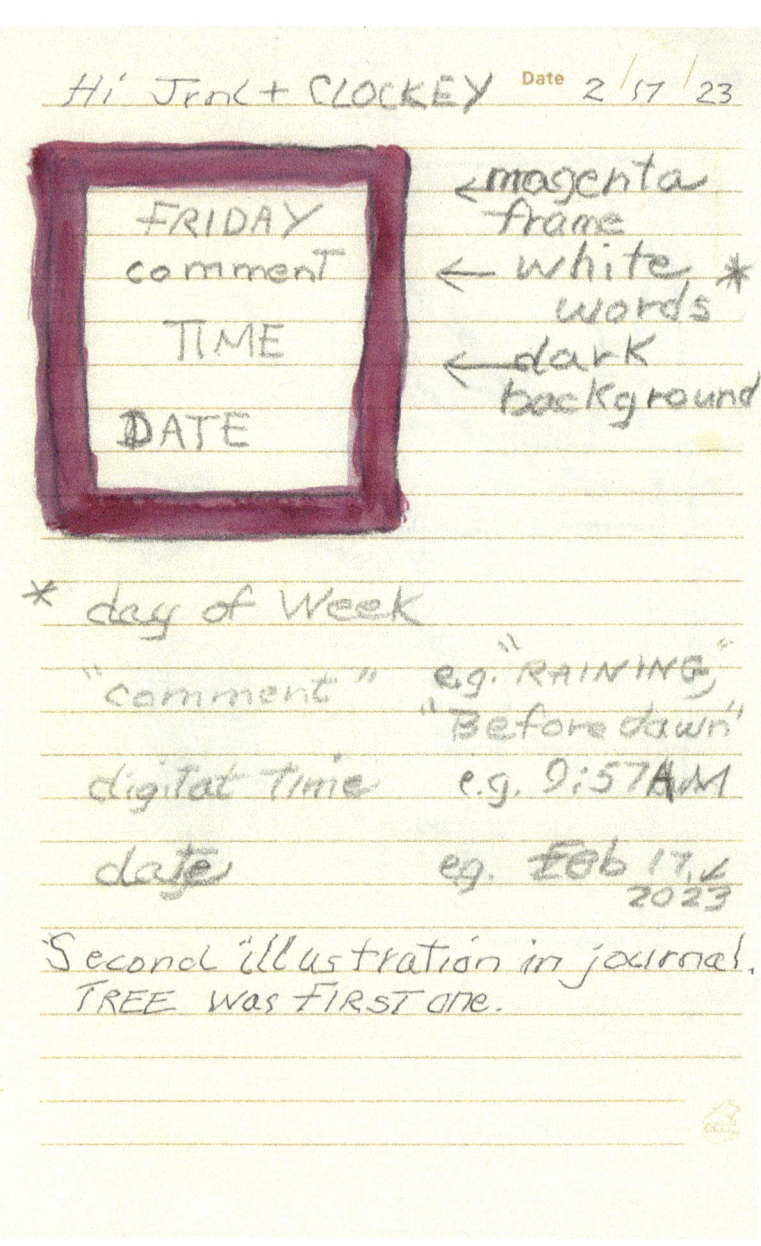

*"Clockey"* (Mom's journal)

My aunt texts to tell me she and her husband will come to visit the next day.

Over breakfast, I say, "Mom, I have a surprise for you."

She looks at me expectantly.

"Your sister is coming to visit today."

Her mouth drops open, and her eyes widen for a full four seconds.

*"Wow. Martha all that Covid,"* she says, meaning that even though her sister has been isolating since 2020 due to the Covid-19 pandemic, she is coming to visit. They arrive wearing K-95 masks. We have another party. This time, my mom stays in bed.

She tells the story of the car accident she was in on her way back to college in Harrisonburg from Richmond in 1958. She and five other students hired a taxi. The taxi veered off the road and struck a stone wall when the driver tried to straighten it. Two of the students died. My mom had a sprained ankle and a bump on her head. I've heard the story from my grandfather several times; he woke up in the night at the time of the crash and knew something was wrong. I've never heard my mom tell it, but she was so nervous during the only driving class she gave me when I was fifteen that it took me another ten years to get my license.

My brother shows her how to get around her neighborhood on Google Maps. She shows him where she goes on walks, new stores on MacArthur Avenue, *"the patio."*

Lots of people send flowers.

During the night my mom can't keep her eyes off the sprinkler system on the ceiling. It has a little green light that flashes constantly, or as she writes, *"blinks itself all night."* She makes up a song (to the tune of "Twinkle, Twinkle Little Star")

*"Twinkle Sprinkle
Sprinkler Star
I know you know
who you are."*

The med tech comes in at 5:30 am. It's perfect timing for my mom to pee. The med tech asks her something (maybe, "Can you stand up?" or "Can you wipe yourself?"), and my mom says, *"So far. Everything 'so far.'"*

She becomes frantic about us finding stuff in the house to take with us: the wedding ring from her marriage with my brother's father, a diamond necklace that was hers when she was young, a charm bracelet that has fallen behind the dresser, a watch that belonged to her father, an abalone shell, a silver cane, a green plush coat. She writes intricate, sometimes inscrutable notes about where we might find things. We do our best.

Her surgeon, Polly, comes to see her. They met in 2000, when my mom was first diagnosed with breast cancer, and have become friends. Polly and I like each other immediately.

We meet the hospice team. The chaplain tells us my mom is "in acceptance" and we should also be. We should let her talk about the past, not correct her, but journey with her. The hospice nurse tells me that once cancer reaches the brain, the decline can be quick. The hospice social worker tells us about anticipatory grief.

My brother and my sister-in-law pack to fly back to California. *"I happy you my son's soul mate,"* my mom tells my sister-in-law.

I find the laundry room and do the laundry.

She says she hasn't seen my body since I was twelve or thirteen and asks to see me naked. Before I change into my pajamas I go to stand by her bed, turning on the yellow lamplight. *"Oh, you have beautiful body. Beautiful woman body. You breasts still nice."*

*Woman in Wheelchair Making Valentine*

*"Good morning Journal,*
*Happy Valentine's day everybody,"* my mom writes.

I paint a valentine for her that says, "I love you, Mom," like I used to when I was little.

Using my watercolors, she makes a Valentine for her husband on one of my postcard papers. *"He'll want something to hold in his hand."*

I paint her.

She is getting better at standing and turning from her wheelchair, and her language is better, but I think she is also getting weaker and more tired. There's something that can fool you about seeming improvement.

She gets a bath. She is resistant to the idea of a bath and especially to changing the gown from the nursing home. She loves it because it has a pocket on the front. When the hospice aide tells her it can be a sponge bath and that she can sit on the closed toilet seat, my mom accepts. I hear her say, *"Oh, that's wonderful."* The hospice aide tells me she begins each bath by placing a very warm washcloth on the person's chest. She changes my mom into her purple nightgown from home, and I put the new blue sheets with white flowers on her bed.

The next day, my mom decides she wants to go to the Valentine's Day party at the assisted living community. She calls her husband later to say she had a good time!

"2/16/23

*Hi jrnl, a morning dream about I am lucid.*

*I'm at the next door neighbor's house wearing Robert E. Lee uniform and boots and think I'll walk home. Twice I gently fall down on the sidewalk. My plan was to show how I could get there and go up the steps to my house in those boots! I didn't get there though. I guess a dream fall is safer than one here that's a real fall but I'm still 'Fall Risk'."*

Her husband tells me he had a dream. He dreamt of a place with lots of stairs going down with different landings. He and I are there together, and my mom is ahead, going down the stairs. We keep trying to call her, but she can't seem to hear us and just continues down the stairs.

## 17 February

The assisted living community decides to name the hospice suite "Sunshine."

Outside room #112 is a plaque with my mom's name. She enjoys seeing it. She sorts through some cards of saints she wants to give to the hospice chaplain. She's very tired and has some pain in her side and back. She has lymphedema in her ankles now. They are heavy for her to lift onto the bed.

She dreams that I pee in her wheelchair, and she is helping me.

*"Maybe my soul will go around and around until it finds a cat."*

"The day red birds appeared at South window! Karen said 'Look at red bird!' Bird is a male cardinal Va. state bird. 'Hi mom' to Hazel, who passed already, so, I'll say 'hi' to Hazel out little south window nesting in old tree."
(Mom's journal entry and drawing.)

When my sister-in-law sees a cardinal, she thinks of it as a visit from her mother.

*"And sunset glow coral, pink, orange, in both windows last a half hour of <u>color</u>!"*
(Mom's journal entry and drawing.)

The other window in my mom's Sunshine bedroom faces West. From her bed, she sees this bench, the path, and trees.

## 18 February

My mom wakes up and tells the nurse about how her daddy said, *"Everybody gotta die."*

Jimmy Carter, US president from 1977 to 1981, has also just gone into hospice care. I read my mom an article about him from the BBC news site. She punctuates her listening with *"I remember that."*

By the time King Charles' coronation rolls around (she would have loved the pomp and circumstance, the pageantry) she is no longer interested in current events.

I take her for a walk around the grounds in her wheelchair. It is a quarter-mile walk. We sit at the bench that she can see from her window, and she is able to situate herself in the outside world in relation to what she sees from her room with a view. I am glad we are able to do it, and she seems to enjoy feeling the sun.

There is a serious problem with the call bells. At dinner, it takes forty-five minutes for someone to come. "OK, they are busy," I think. At 12:54 a.m. I wake up to hear her screaming my name (her voice is weak, though), and it has been an hour since she pulled the cord. They say it is a miscommunication from the previous shift, but just before 4 a.m., I wake up again to her calling. Neither her cord nor her bracelet call button work, so that needs to be sorted out. They tell me they will put her on a two-hour watch.

This is not a good omen on the last day before I return to Spain.

Friends come in the morning to drive me to the airport. They bring a set of sixteen jumbo-size crayons for my mom to use while I am gone. My son is returning home from Berlin, and I need to be there to receive him. His paternal grandfather is dying as well. I made a deal with him to wait to see my son.

The hospice nurse will let me know when my mom's condition worsens, and I will return.

On the plane from Richmond to New York JFK, I feel like I am in a mystic forest of cotton candy. The clouds tell me that I need to get back soon. The action is where my mom is.

*"2/20/23*
*Hi Jrnl,*
*I slept pretty good*
*off and on after 9 pm*
*through 9 am Monday.*
*after I ate all breakfast*

*If I was wakeful I was thoughtful; even wondering if I might visit home one last time.*

*Maybe someone will bring my husband here Friday <u>or</u> Sat or Sunday.*

*OK, now I'm ready for bathroom + toilet so I can get back in bed.*

*Bell chords and calls still not all working, So I hope someone will come back very soon. She said she will."*

My mom writes this journal entry the day after I go back to Spain.

## 22 February

We FaceTime with my mom.

She is more tired. Quieter. She is drawing the caregivers using the new crayons. I will recognize some of them, she says.

Title: illustration Care "peeps" (My mom's drawing of the caregivers.)

She tells my partner and me it's nice we can take care of each other. Says she dreamt she was home and sleeping with her husband for a little while.

*"You left your spirit in the room next door.*

I go with my son to see his grandfather. He is very thin. He fell out of his hospital bed and doesn't really want to eat. My son wonders if it is worth keeping people alive.

## 25 February

My mom tells the assisted living community she doesn't want visitors or phone calls; she just wants rest. Finally, someone puts me through, and I am able to talk to her; I feel relieved and happy. She tells me they are putting a bird feeder outside her big window, where she sees the bench.

*At home garden*

The hospice nurse contacts me sooner than I expected; she tells me my mom is declining and that I should try to come back. I book a ticket to depart on March 6th and return on the 26th. The next day, she sends an email: "There's been a change in condition with your mom. She is very confused; her speech is slurred. Her fingertips and toes are dark, and she has mild grayness under her bottom lip. No pain or shortness of breath. (Our on-call nurse went out there). I will see her tomorrow. I know it's short notice, but I think you should come down as soon as you can."

I manage to change my ticket to March 1st. I have to leave very early in the morning and fly via Paris. My friend Ursula's son is on the plane from Barcelona to Paris, an uncanny synchronicity. He is on his way back to his family in Japan. I am back in the mystic forest of cotton candy.

My best friend from high school meets me at the Richmond airport. She takes me out to lunch and then drives me to the assisted living community. It's dark when we arrive and cold outside. My mom is sleeping; she seems smaller. I get into bed with her, the warm, wiggly hospice bed. She tells my friend I used to sleep in bed with her when I was little.

In the morning, my mom decides this is her last day. *"Let's take a tour and bust this joint."*

She has coffeecake, coffee, ice cream, Ensure, and milk for breakfast. "At the end, it's normal for them to want only liquids. She's listening to her body," the hospice nurse reassures me by text.

She goes back to sleep. When she wakes up, we take the quarter-mile walk. When we come around to the entrance, she refuses to go inside. She insists that this is her last day. She says a van will pick her up, and she will be cremated. Says her momma was singing to her. Makes me take off her wedding band and put it on my finger. *"Bye, my husband. I go Home."*

Somehow, I convince her to go back to the room. Joy, my mom's neighbor and walking companion, and Polly coincide as visitors. My mom sits in her wheelchair in a delirious state while the three of us talk. She finally gets into bed and sleeps. When she wakes up, she talks to Joy normally.

The hospice nurse pays a visit. "It will be like a roller coaster," she tells me. My mom's oxygen, blood pressure, and heart rate are all normal.

The hospice chaplain visits again. "She is in and out. This is her time. She is in both worlds. Let her be alone to treasure this time. She wants to be free from attachments to meet her maker. Let her set the agenda. Don't correct her. She asked me to pray that her transition is peaceful. She asked me to pray for her soul to be at rest. She is not in the same world that you are in. She is with the people here AND the people there."

She tells me twice that not only do I have my father's ears, but I have his eyes as well.

She enjoys three segments of the mandarin orange I brought from Spain.

# 4 March

*"I bet Polly will come visit you in Spain."*

"That would be great," I say. "It's so nice that you are leaving her to me."

*"Nice to know life goes on."*

"The show must go on," I say, "but you'll be in a different show."

*"Maybe I'll come back as a genius and work in cyber-security."*

Today, she mostly sleeps, coughs, and complains that the inside of her mouth is bothering her. Medication has helped the lymphedema in her ankles; they've gone back to their normal size.

Another friend from high school comes to visit. Together, we take the quarter-mile walk and put birdseed in my mom's new feeder. When we get back to the suite, we are talking and laughing; my mom wants us to come into her room so she can be part of it. She asks my friend if his mom is still here.

"No," he tells her, "She died in September."

My mom is happy that his mom will be wherever she is going. Surprisingly to me, my mom doesn't want a funeral; she tells us we can hold a memorial at *"the patio."*

## 5 March

*"Please, please, pretty please, let my soul go free."*

In the middle of the night, my mom spills her cup of water. The caretakers get her up and change the sheets and her nightgown. She talks to them normally: no delirium, regular language syntax. I hear her say to the clock, *"Happy birthday Lin."* Her brother would have been 91, like my son's grandfather. Lin died in 2020, on the same day as George Floyd.

In the evening, I meet a childhood friend of my mom's who comes to visit. My mom is excited to see her, but the excitement turns into agitation. She wants to participate in the conversation and be understood, but it is difficult for her.

*"Monitors Mothers Motivation delete memory embellishment sockets plugs eliminate dot coms B. and A. told me you gave them some vertigo points. B. told me you took a Bellevue break prompt. Passwords. Cut. All lines established for your removal of the clickers (Bed controls?) R. deletes.com flowers and forsythia blessings. Chocolate. Reverie bundles. Furkle the birds. Karen blesses me with her thanks of being born to her father Jay. A blessing is invoked. And green cats from hats and Sam I am and passwords require dot com and delicate almond skin colors of the world and delicate leaves on vine and grinches have cats and hats and J. and R. have cats and hats and Noah has cats and hats. And endless coughing and hats are welcome in my world and erratic. Buttons and enhancing colors of ribbon that match our clothing or sweaters, girls. Hillbillies and golf courses and recreational animals from the jungle. Numerous legless and two carrots. Cats, stilts, and hatboxes. The purple password that lets the musical staff go away with the kitty. N. loves me - I just got it in a message about those clickers he flourishes. It's just taking so long for all those gold alerts to come. I'm just waiting for the beautiful colors. It takes so long to do all these deletes. The Catalan morsels are coming. I'm gonna quit."*

"Quit what?"

"Quit morseling. That's all I've got over here is that morseling. Now what's next to grow? I got that stop sign out. It's all morseling."

I learn online that sometimes delirium is part of the final stages of dying.

## 6 March

She tells me I have style and talks about buying calico and paisley at the Miller & Rhoads department store when *"we"* were kids (she and I). There is a moment of lucidity, *"You're wearing a lovely dress."* Since then, it's been mostly delirium.

I help her make a shadow box to hang outside her door. All the residents have one. Usually, the activities director makes it after the resident explains a bit about who they are, where they are from, and what they have enjoyed doing. My mom wants to make her own. She's won prizes at the state fair for her intricate button mandalas and designs; now, it's like working with a two-year-old. She manages to arrange some butterfly stickers and ribbons. She glues five brown wooden heart-shaped buttons. I can imagine her as a small child discovering arts and crafts and her creative potential.

*"I don't much like family, but maybe it was because with Granny, there were all these relatives and you had to know who everyone was, and me and my cousin just wanted to play. All these relatives who knew who you were."*

*"I will never walk again."* She tells me three times that she will never walk again. The third time she says, *"I was so startled when I realized I'll never walk again."*

*Mom's in there.* (The first window on the right is hers, the second is mine.)

I take the quarter-mile walk and paint the view of Mom's room from the bench outside.

She's in there coughing.

I hear her say, *"It's hard. Dying is hard today. I don't know why."*

I'm reading about chesty secretions when a friend calls me from Vermont. She tells me about her grandmother's delirium, how she was blowing on something imaginary. Maybe a candle, my friend thought.

"What are you blowing on, Ooma?" she asked.

Her grandmother answered in Polish, Lithuanian, and German.

"Ooma, tell it in English," my friend coaxed.

*"Dandelion."*

My mom wants me to buy a bouquet for her husband with one red ruby rose and a lot of lavender daisies and white daisies. Their fortieth wedding anniversary is in three weeks.

We enjoy seeing birds at the feeder, and mostly, it's a normal day.

She says goodbye to a friend by phone.

When the caregiver asks her, "Aren't you gonna sit with your daughter at the table?" my mom decides to get out of bed. She wants to write in her journal but winds up reading it instead, reviewing everything she has written and drawn since she's been in the assisted living community.

We both sleep for seven hours straight.

## 8 March

She sleeps more before breakfast, then eats while my stepsister visits. She sees a cardinal at the bird feeder. She returns to her delirium.

She's concerned she'll have to write the cause of death on her own death certificate.

She sleeps again, wearing a silk eye mask I brought with me. She loves the dark it provides. She also loves my weighted, heart-shaped beanbag "eye pillow". Since my head injury, I sometimes use it to rest my brain. Now it's hers and has a name: *"Braveheart."* These two objects offer more comfort than I could have imagined.

*"I reckon everyone should have a live-in daughter."*

*Cardinal at Feeder*

## 9 March

My mom has been at the assisted living community for four weeks, which is also one month, since it's February 9th to March 9th. *"That's about how long I expected to be here."*

"You never know," I respond, "It could be another month."

For breakfast, she has some apple streusel baked by her childhood friend. The regular breakfast comes early, and we sit at the table to eat it. I tell her about the drizzly weather and that 8° Celsius is 46° Fahrenheit. I read about the UK, the US, and Australia's 2032 plan to have nuclear submarines against China and about the Chinese mediation between Iran and Saudi Arabia.

After breakfast, she goes back to sleep; she wakes up a bit when Joy comes to visit. "Are you ready?" Joy asks. This is a question Joy wishes she had asked her husband. My mom says she's ready but it's up to God. She seems to be discovering that letting her soul go free is not entirely up to her.

She sleeps again until 1:30 p.m., then eats all her lunch with coconut cream pie for dessert. She reads letters that have arrived from friends. Some people send "Get Well" cards. She sleeps again.

She is coughing. "Did she have the Covid test?" asks the caregiver.

"She had it yesterday," I say. "It's just end-of-life coughing."

*"Karen, blessing. Stay. Don't go. Sit. Sit."*

So, I am here, sitting.

## 10 March

A brown thrush comes to the bird feeder, then a blue jay, some tiny finches, and a red-bellied woodpecker. The eastern towhee is on the ground again and more than seven robins. And of course, the squirrels.

There is lots of coughing and the hospice nurse gives my mom some medicine for secretions. Her oxygen level is 92.5.

*Robins know the rain is coming*

Birds enjoy the seeds.
I think it will rain later.
Robins look for worms.
(haiku)

*Snacks*

This is the bedside table where she keeps her snacks - Lorna Doone cookies, Oreos, Nutter Butters, Fig-Newtons, graham crackers, bananas - all provided by the assisted living community.

## 11 March

*"Some people on the Other Side are welcoming me with those things I call cornstalks. Tomato bean cornstalks. The triple succotash, I call it."*

It has been thirty days since I first came to Richmond: ten days here, ten days in Spain, ten days here again.

My mom and her sister say their mom appears to them as a mockingbird. On the phone, she tells her sister, *"If you see a mockingbird, welcome it. May as well welcome it as to being fussy."*

During the night, I hear banging that sounds like it's coming from another room, not our suite. My body feels too heavy to get up and see what it is. At 5:30 a.m. I hear the med tech asking, "What are you doing here?" My mom has somehow managed to get into her wheelchair on her own and is facing the wall, muttering and delirious, trying to pull the plug of the hospital bed out of the wall.

It's daylight savings time. We see a lovely pink morning sky. We change *Master Clock* manually.

I go to brunch with some friends. I ask the caregiver to keep an eye on my mom, as she is delirious and got out of her bed last night. I must be famished; I finish off a plate of eggs Benedict and another of croissant French toast.

When I get back to the assisted living community, the caretaker seeks me out. She found my mom in the bathroom, in her wheelchair, on her own. She had opened a package of cotton face pads and was washing them in the sink.

My mom is agitated for the rest of the day and is given anti-anxiety medication. Her hands can't stop moving. I play mantras on my ukulele for her; I am trying to calm myself. I give her my foot so that she has something to hold on to. She gives one foot and then the other a very deep massage. She lifts and lowers her hands as if in surrender. *"It's like quilting!"* She exclaims. *"Why would anyone wash cotton balls?"*

## 13 March

She is delighted I am here.
    She fidgets with *"Braveheart"*.
    *"It's amazing what hands can do."*
    She's busy hunting stars.

*My mom's self-portrait*

She wants her wedding ring back on again.

The hospice nurse consults with the doctor and prescribes a medication called Seroquel. It will help with the delirium and the agitation. "Your mom will be calmer, more herself."

On Wednesdays, a hairdresser comes to the assisted living community; my mom is eager to have her hair done. I schedule her an early appointment so she won't have to wait long. Nonetheless, she is not the first. We wait. My mom gets agitated. Suddenly, the med tech appears and says she has medicine for my mom. It seems urgent. I am impressed with her efficiency. During her haircut, my mom looks like she is falling asleep. When it is over, I wheel her back to the room. She falls asleep right away after I get her into bed, which is not easy; it's as if her body weighs more.

When she wakes up, she is lethargic. Her speech is unclear.

I learn that the medicine she got before the haircut was the Seroquel. I say no to more.

Word arrives from Spain that my son's grandfather has died. My mom met him at my wedding. *"Oh no,"* she says when I tell her. *"That is sad."* She knows how much he meant to me. *"You must go back and pay homage."*

"No, Mom. I'm staying right here with you."

Later in the night, when I am helping her to the bathroom, she is relieved that I am still here. *"I don't know how much I need you until I need you."*

## 15 March

A friend I know from Yogaville comes to sing for my mom. My mom recognizes some of the hymns from the Presbyterian church she grew up in. My friend and I chant, "Om Shanti." My mom learns this means, "May you be at peace." She has her eyes closed and confuses my friend's voice with mine. *"I never heard you sing soprano; it's gorgeous."*

She throws off her covers and is lying in the sunlight.

My mom is fading.

I am in the land of the living.

For dinner, she has canned peaches and is able to express that she is cranky due to pain.

*"Oh, I've been dreaming about my Tylenol,"* she tells the med tech at 5:30 a.m.

## 16 March

Her husband comes to visit. She asks him if he likes her hair. "It looks wonderful," he says. He tells her he bought a transport chair so that he can come and visit more often. She tells him she needs to let go. He is visibly crestfallen. "You are free to go at any time, and you will go with love," he tells her when he leaves.

She's concerned about who she can trust but is able to calm down when I tell her we are safe here.

At 5.30 a.m. she tells the med tech that she is ready to let go. "I miss my mom so much," the med tech replies. "Don't let go, you stay as long as you can."

*"Mothers let go. Their souls become other mothers,"* says my mom by way of consolation.

On the quarter-mile walk, I see a twisted entangled small tree. Now it has purple buds on its grey limbs. One of the assisted living community staff sees me contemplating it. "It's called weeping cherry."

*Weeping Cherry*

## 17 March

My mom tells me she learned about the eastern towhee bird when she met my father. His cat had one in its mouth, and they helped it get away. Usually, the towhees are on the ground where she can't see them. Today, one lands on the feeder. I hear her shout "Too-hi!" and realize the name is onomatopoeic. In Native-American folklore, the towhee is said to be a guide to the afterlife. Its red eyes are thought to be a link to the spirit world.

*Towhee male and female*

Thanks to the Seroquel episode, I realize that part of my mom's delirium has to do with having pain she is unable to locate or verbalize. With the hospice nurse, we decide to schedule oxycodone, rather than just Tylenol, every twelve hours.

It works. When she wakes up and is taken to pee, she feels less pain. Her mouth pain disappears. The pull-on "brief" bothers her less when it is pulled up, and she lifts her own feet while it's being changed. She stands up from and sits down in the wheelchair with less effort. *"It's easier to 'plop' into my chair."*

One of her biggest concerns has been the fate of her cat. She and her husband adopted a declawed black cat who turned out to have been a feral kitten. They nearly returned her to the animal shelter but kept her out of compassion, believing no one else would. After eight years, she is still skittish and shy, responding only to my mom and her husband, running to the bedroom to hide whenever anyone comes to the door, and occasionally, even biting the hand that feeds her. During her delirium, my mom decided the cat is so afraid because of some thorns, which are stuck in her forehead, underneath her fur. With a bit of Vaseline, someone can remove the thorns, and the cat will be okay. Now my mom conflates herself with the cat, saying the thorns under her own forehead skin hurt less.

I read to her from the Bellevue Times newsletter about alley bartering and the great horned owls in Bryan Park.

When the med tech arrives, my mom asks for *"the Winter medicine,"* her name for the new pain reliever.

It's Spring now. The hospice nurse and I see a rabbit in the grass.

My flight back is six days away.

I sing the Om Shanti chant. "*Thank you, Shanti, for a loving daughter, and for protecting everything she doth love.*"

Her oxygen level is 95.

The Sufi mystic Llewellyn Vaughan-Lee teaches that when you die, the light of your eyes meets the light of your soul.

A neighbor sends some flowers from her yard.

*Forsythia*

*The path.*

 I change my return flight to May 15th, the day after Mother's Day.
*"You sure leaving it long."*
 We see a purple finch and a mockingbird at the feeder.
 On the quarter-mile walk, I see a deer and the wind in the trees.
 Joy brings my mom's husband to visit.
 My mom thanks me for helping her recognize her limits.

*This is the chair at the foot of my mom's bed.*

She tells me my soul and my brother's soul looked to her to be our momma and chose our fathers as well.

"*I wonder who my soul will choose, or maybe I'll be a cat.*"

## 24 March

At 9 a.m., she begins a button project. I don't know what she imagines she is doing, but in practice, it involves taking the buttons out of their plastic bags, spreading some glue on paper, and returning the buttons to their plastic bags. She spends two hours on her own with this project, then asks me to put the buttons and the glued paper away in the drawer.

When the hospice nurse arrives, my mom tells her she's not ready to leave.

On the quarter-mile walk, I see a fox.

My best friend from high school visits, and we walk in the nearby woods. We have dinner at an Indian restaurant and bring back some rice pudding and honey balls for my mom.

She seems like she's in a reverie, and I say so. *"Yes! A reverie!"*

*"Wheels within wheels for me on what is now March 25"*

With this journal entry, my mom marks the beginning of several days of *"worlds within worlds."* There are *"lights within lights,"* *"poops within poops,"* and *"tears within tears."* I am *"resourceful within resourceful."* She also randomly repeats *"a kind word"*, as if maybe that's all that is needed.

*Colors within Colors*

I'm testing out how the watercolors look on the paper, and she says, *"It's colors within colors.*

It's raining.

My son tells me this shouldn't be my life; I should get out and do something.

The med tech spent nine months with her mom in hospice. "You need to keep your hind parts in there."

My mom tells me to put her journal in the drawer.

She goes into the reverie again. "What do you see in the reverie?" I ask.

*"I don't know how to say it. It's love attempting to be love."*

I take her on the quarter-mile walk. She wears her maroon cape over her turquoise flowered nightgown. I show her the tulips that have bloomed. We go into the gazebo, which is just off the path. She wants to get out of her wheelchair and sit with me. *"I want to sit on the bench with my daughter."* We sit, and I hold her. She is warm. *"Thank you for loving me."*

## 26 March

This was the day I was going to fly home.
    I hear her in her room:
    *"Oh, bright sunshine,*
    *thank you.*
    *Thank you for another day*
    *and another bird.*
    *Thank you."*

"Yesterday was my flight home," I say.
    *"Oh! Thank you for staying. Why do you love me so much?"*
    "Because you're my mom."
    She sits with the watercolors, mixing colors to make magenta.
    I order larger pull-on briefs. She's gained weight.
    *"I'm so glad I don't have to pull that cord."*

*Window bug.*

(This insect is on my mom's window)

## 28 March

*"Sometimes I'm on a little green train, and I'm going either East or West, and sometimes I'm on it, and sometimes I'm not,"* she tells the med tech.

Jonathan the Juggler arrives and surprises her with a private juggling and magic show. She has attended his events around the city since he began and has known him since he was a child. He's just a little older than my brother. *"Next time you come, you ride in on your unicycle, juggling those flames."*

She has me bring her wheelchair over to the sink so that she can wash two empty coffee creamer containers.

She wants to go home in a transport chair so she can say goodbye to the cat.

*My mom's crayon drawing, "Spring I paint you."*

I have never seen
Spring unfold in quite this way.
Flowers bloom and fade.

I write a haiku after going on the quarter-mile walk.

*Mom's in bed. Loves her quilt.*
(This is the view from the red-striped chair)

She has a bath and sleeps all day until Polly comes to visit. She makes it to the table to eat lunch, which is dinner. She thinks everything is hilarious. Polly departs, and my mom goes back to bed.

I talk to my brother on speakerphone, and our mom listens.

I take a longer walk in the neighborhood and end it with the quarter-mile walk. When I pass my mom's room, I look in her window. She sees me and is agitated, *"Come, come!"* I return quickly to her room. *"I go!"* she shouts. I put my hands on her to calm her; her breathing seems different. I wonder if she was given medicine while I was on my walk. I wonder what the night will bring.

In the middle of the night, she wakes up and says she wants to change the plan of *"Letting my soul go free"* to *"Let go and let God."*

It's two months now since she went to the emergency room.

I order the anniversary bouquet from her neighborhood florist.

We see the rabbit from her window.

*Our little breakfast nook with March calendar.*

On April 1st, I go to change the calendar.
*"Can I do it?"*
I lift the calendar down to wheelchair level, and my mom turns the page to the new month.

She gets up for lunch: egg salad, onion rings, potato soup, cherry pie. She breaks into song:
*"Can she make a cherry pie, Billy Boy, Billy Boy,*
*Can she make a cherry pie, charming Billy?*
*She can make a cherry pie, quick as you can wink an eye,*
*For she's a young thing and cannot leave her mother."*

The azalea bush outside her window has bloomed. The flowers are big and pink.

There is a storm, with wind and lightning.

*Mom's Worldview*

My friend Damon tells me I am doing a big Mitzvah. "Do I get a prize?" I ask.

"Yeah," he says, "you'll get a baseball cap."

Damon tells my mom he remembers her being sweet to him when he was a child.

At 9:30 p.m. I take her to the bathroom, and suddenly, she starts to cry. "It's okay," I say.

*"I'm sorry. It's hard,"* she cries.

I hug her. *"It's kind for Damon to say what he said."* She cries.

*"It's burny,"* she says.

"Do you have pain?" I ask.

*"No, it's grief."*

*Fluffy White Flowers*

    Every time I take the quarter-mile walk now, something new is in bloom. This one began as light green brushes and transformed into fluffy white flowers. I have no idea what it is.

Today is her ruby anniversary. She and her husband have been married for forty years. Was she holding on for this date? In her last journal entry, she writes:

"*Hi Journal,*

*Tonight I have been thinking and hoping for my husband's daughter to do certain actual things that help me know what I can ask her to do.*

*One is to buy 4 packages of UKROP's hot cross buns: 1 to freeze for my husband when he want more. 2 packages to bring here to my room. One he can have any time he is ready!*

*Husband, I love you. Your*

*Wife.*"

The neighborhood florist goes to my mom's husband's house in person to bring him the bouquet.

*"Hello world, thank you for being out there,"* I hear my mom say.

I take the quarter-mile walk and see the fox with three kits. I see two bluebirds. When my mom and my aunt see bluebirds, they think of their father.

Polly brings her granddaughters to meet my mom.

My mom's husband comes with Joy for an anniversary celebration. Joy provides sparkling grape juice and roasted Virginia peanuts. To give them some time alone together, we take the quarter-mile walk. We sit on the bench she sees from her window. They can see us, but we can't see them. Suddenly, her husband's silhouette appears at the window, banging with his cane. My mom has to pee and is distressed. We head back to the room, and I help her. Her husband sees how calm and present I am with her. My mom gets overwhelmed when there is too much input. Three tumors are in her brain.

I take the long walk in the neighborhood again and come across a sweetshrub bush. My grandfather had one in his front yard. I recall the bluebirds I saw this morning. "I think it means Grandad - your dad - is with you." The memory of her marriage to her husband in my grandfather's house comes to me, and I tell her.

She looks at me.

*"It's all just magical, magical, magical."*

## 3 April

My mom has a fearful and delirious night. Too many worlds within worlds.

In the morning, she gets excited when she sees what looks like a tiny sparrow on the feeder. Then another, a red-breasted one, appears. Everyone else I know believes their deceased relatives appear as birds, so when I learn the name of this songbird, I decide my mom will come to me as a house finch.

The hospice nurse discovers us having breakfast in my room while the rest of the suite is being cleaned.

The hospice chaplain pays another visit.

The hospice social worker pays another visit.

We have lunch and dinner beside her bed.

Maybe tomorrow I can convince her to sit outside in the sun.

# 4 April

*"Were you aware of all that controversy?"* My mom asks when she wakes up.
"What controversy?"
*"About yourself."*
"What was it?"
*"You had a pink brick in your throat."*
"Oh no! What happened?"
*"Well, you got it out."*

We go outside briefly after breakfast, and she is happy to see a bumblebee.

The neighborhood florist comes to visit with her partner. Their cat, who lives in the florist shop, is on the front page of *The Richmond Times Dispatch*. They've brought the newspaper to show to my mom. She would have loved this news. If she had been home, she would have cut out the article to give to them. She begins screaming and asks them to take the article away. I keep it, thinking later she'll want to see it, but she doesn't.

She is afraid. It takes over ten minutes for her to calm down from the screaming. I pull the cord for help, but no one comes until an hour later. She is given anti-anxiety medication again because of the screaming. For pain, she is on oxycodone only twice a day but also takes medication for seizures and brain swelling, as her cancer has metastasized to her brain. It's as if her brain is giving up, and her mind is trying to find ways to work around her brain, or as if she is trying to get her brain to work with her mind.

During the night, she is hot and throws off the sheet and the chuck pad.

*"Does anyone scream with pain?"* she asks the next morning.
"Some people do," I say, "Do you have pain?"
She doesn't know.

In mid-April, my high school is celebrating its fiftieth reunion. Last November, my partner and I bought tickets to travel to Richmond. My partner has never met my mom or been to the city where I grew up. The anniversary reunion provided a pretext for returning so soon after my visit last May.

I told my mom we were coming and said we could walk in the ravine again. *"Maybe you can do that with your partner."*

Now her response makes sense.

In February, when I flew for the first time, we did not know what would be happening in April. Would I go home, and we'd return together for the anniversary reunion? Would my mom be alive?

The flights are non-refundable, and the dates cannot be changed. Over the last few weeks, we have been waiting to decide what to do. Now it's clear I will still be here. We decide he will use his ticket. I am living in the assisted living community and won't leave my mom; he cannot stay here.

Polly offers to host him at her house. She takes me to see it. She lives on a man-made lake. Azaleas and pink and white dogwoods are in bloom. We see a hawk and deer.

"I think of cancer cells as early settlers," she tells me. "They send out scouts and try to colonize." She says the cancer cells in my mom's brain were probably already in her bloodstream when she had the mastectomy in 2019.

*Grass within Grass*

    For some reason, this patch of yellow-y grass is growing in the grass my mom sees from her window. The colors appeal to me so I paint it. The next day, the lawn mower comes, and it is gone. *"The man who mows our lawn has a metal truck."* my mom says.

## 6 April

She sleeps through the night from 8:30 p.m. until 3:30 a.m., waking up for the bathroom and her Ensure. The med tech wakes her for Tylenol at 5:30 a.m. At 7 a.m., she wakes again to go to the bathroom and begins to cry. *"I don't know anything."* She doesn't seem to know where she is. She doesn't want my hand on her back, stroking her head, or even combing her hair, which she usually enjoys. I suspect she is having more physical pain. I explain to her that as part of this process, she will have more pain and that I will ask the hospice nurse to prescribe more medicine. It's the first time she seems to understand the connection between the pain and the medicine, and she wants me to ask the hospice nurse right away. The med tech wonders if she needs morphine.

For some reason, one of the hardest parts about accompanying my mom is realizing that this is HER journey. It seems like that would be obvious, but I feel so close to it that it's not.

In the afternoon, she wakes up from a nap and has a peanut butter and jelly sandwich. My friend in Vermont writes a haiku:

Stop and feel the Sun.
Peanut Butter and Jelly.
Assist the Living.

*The Vines Were Wisteria*

The winter vines turn out to be wisteria.
*"Expectations are on me now to die already and get it done with."*
It's a full moon.

And, of course, there are the squirrels squirreling around! Lots of people tell me what pests squirrels are. They give hints on how to keep them away from the feeder.

*Squirrel at feeder.*

However, I want you to know that if you know someone who is housebound but has a window that faces a bird feeder, squirrels provide constant entertainment, as well as engagement with the outside world. They just need someone able-bodied to keep putting seeds in the feeder.

*Squirreling around I*

*Squirreling around II*

*Squirreling around III*

## 7 April

My mom wakes up and eats pound cake with cherries.

She goes back to sleep and wakes up for her medication, then begins to scream and cry. I tell her it's normal to be afraid and have more pain and remind her that the hospice nurse is coming today to help figure that out. *"The medicines come and come, but the pain comes back."*

I suspect the pain creates her anxiety. She is no longer delirious.

The hospice nurse agrees to schedule oxycodone every eight hours.

At mid-day, my mom is curled up into a ball. She refuses anti-anxiety medication. I go out, and when I return three hours later, she is still curled. When she sees me, she is relieved. *"You've been gone long."*

She complains that no one has checked on her, but there is a piece of mail on her tray that has been opened. She begins talking about *"rain within rain"* and stopping all the *"withins the withins"* so I ask the med tech to try the anti-anxiety medication again. Again, she refuses. She curls up again.

She eats a hot cross bun and curls up again.

I tell her I am grateful to her for who I am. She tells me she is also grateful for who I am: *"Resourceful within resourceful."*

In the evening, she is still curled up. She chats a tiny bit and re-curls. She wants to refuse the evening medicine as well. When I tell her she may have a lot of pain, she decides to take it.

It's her legal right to refuse medication.

## 8 April

I wonder if she refuses the meds because, somehow, the pain and madness are preferable to sleep and peace.

She wakes up twice in the night to pee and has a snack each time: Ensure at 1:30 a.m. and rice pudding at 5:30 a.m. She eats grits and waffles for breakfast, then tells me to get her journal out of the drawer so that she can write in it. Instead, she looks through it.

The activities director asks if she wants to come out and play bingo. She declines.

*"If I could just find a constant, comfortable feeling, I could just let go"*

The caregiver tells me my mom's process is the most bizarre she has ever seen. The hospice nurse says her case is very interesting.

"It's a big, big roller coaster," she says, "I've seen this happen before where they are just up and down constantly. Have you thought about staying with a friend for a few days and nights and seeing how your mom does?" I tell her my partner is coming on Tuesday. I could try at least one night. Maybe it's a good idea.

My mom eats most of her lunch.

I take a walk in the nearby woods and to the big grocery store. I buy a butterfly-shaped helium balloon for my mom and a yellow dishtowel decorated with poppies for our kitchen area. It feels silly to buy the dishtowel, but I've been using a cloth napkin from the assisted living community, and the dishtowel is pretty. It's eye level to my mom's wheelchair, and when she notices it, I am happy I bought it. *"That beautiful!"*

She thinks the balloon is funny but tells me to take it out of her room and keep it in the common area.

The oxycodone is on schedule every eight hours, and she is definitely calmer.

*Helium butterfly*

My mom wonders if the butterfly will pop.
"No," I say, "it will probably just lose its helium slowly."
*"Oh,"* she says. *"Slowly. Like us."*

*Kitchen #3*

In the painting, the guest snack basket is on the counter to the left. The new yellow dishtowel with poppies is hanging on the drawer. My kitchen magnets of kitchens are on the refrigerator. The duck was in my room, and I put it on top of the fridge; my mom sees it from her bed and has me put a piece of blue construction paper we saved from the shadow box project under the duck as if it were water.

## Easter Sunday

My mom says she feels like she's going crazy. She talks about letting go. "Is that what you told your mom? To let go?" I ask her.

She is thoughtful, then answers, *"Yes. I wonder what kind of worlds she had. Maybe like this one."*

Easter brunch arrives, crab cakes, corn, and zucchini succotash.

I show her the illustrations in a hardbound copy of *The Little Prince* that I found at her house.

*"I have a dry breath,"* she says.

I go to the Monument Avenue Easter parade. Jonathan the Juggler is there on his unicycle. Someone I know from high school is playing guitar.

At night, my mom tells me she wants her mother to make it easy for her, and that she will help make it easier for me when it's my turn.

*View of Bench.*

This is the view from my mom's bedside of the bench outside.

## 10 April

When she wakes up, she is more lucid but seems a bit weaker.

*"It's easier to live than it is to die."*

We take the quarter-mile walk to her window, and she sees the azaleas of 'her' bush in bloom from the outside.

She eats very little lunch. She stopped eating meat at least three weeks ago. The hospice nurse shows me in the hospice booklet that meat is the first food to go.

My high school friend and I take a walk in the nearby woods. We see a bluebird and a baby squirrel with its mom. There are azaleas in bloom in the woods as well.

*Nearby Woods*

## 11 April

My partner is on his flight now.

I take the quarter-mile walk and put more seed in the bird feeder.

My mom really wants to die today. *"Wish I had dulled eyes."*

When I return from visiting her husband at their house, she grabs my hand and doesn't want me to leave the room.

I leave at 9.30 p.m. to go to the airport with Polly. My mom understands where I am going and why. I ring the bell after midnight to get back into the assisted living community.

My partner wakes up at Polly's house. My mom is still sleeping. I wake her up when breakfast arrives.

In the afternoon, my partner comes to the assisted living community. *"The light in his eyes is still good for loving you,"* she tells me.

Then, something completely unexpected happens: the director of the assisted living community tells me I am no longer allowed to stay here. There was a corporate meeting. I would need to be a resident; I am not. I can stay again when my mom is "actively dying." I ask if I can stay one more night. I break the news to my mom. *"It's their bottom line,"* she mutters.

*"It's all useless,"* my mom declares the next morning. I ask if she will take her medicine today. *"Of course not. What's the point of that?"* She says it just gets even crazier with the anti-anxiety medication, so *"Back it all off."*

She eats some breakfast.

She insists on wiping her own butt.

She is lifting and lowering her hands and screaming about wanting to scream.

Because she is so agitated, I take her on the quarter-mile walk. We see the rabbit.

*"It never ends, and I don't know how to end it."*

The hospice nurse tells me again that it's a roller coaster. My mom's process is very unique.

My partner visits in the afternoon. She tells him she loves him and thanks him for loving me. We leave together; my mom will spend the night on her own for the first time since February.

After forty-three nights of sleeping in the assisted living community, the frogs and nighttime sounds on Polly's lake are like a sound bath.

When I wake up at Polly's house, the sky is pink and reflects in the lake like a tourmaline.

Polly finds moss in the chickadee feeder; someone is making a nest.

I return to the assisted living community at 9 a.m. My mom is sound asleep. Her Ensure is unopened. She wakes up and is happy to see me. She says the med tech told her to take her meds three times a day and try to stay calm. *"So, I say to myself, stay calm and wait for Karen."* She eats all of her breakfast.

"You were hungry," I say.

"See how much energy it takes to stay calm?"

My stepsister comes to visit. Her mom is in hospice care as well now and has been moved to my stepsister's house. She is receiving daily hospice visits. My mom wakes up enough to say hello.

She eats some rice and vegetables and goes back to sleep. I leave at 7:30 p.m.

## 15 April

The next morning, the med tech tells me my mom was screaming and refused breakfast. *"It's not safe here,"* she affirms when I walk into the room.

Today is the anniversary reunion of my high school. I have arranged for people to sit with my mom on two-hour shifts. She says it's unnecessary. *"I'm ready to go."* My stepsister cancels her shift because she needs to be with her own mom.

We have a wonderful time at the event, I reconnect with beloved friends and teachers. I take my partner for a walk in the nearby Hollywood Cemetery, the most beautiful cemetery I have ever visited.

My stepsister's mom dies during the night. I tell my mother that her husband's ex-wife has gone. She seems almost jealous; how did the ex-wife beat her to it? She's been trying so hard to let go. Her husband visits.

My friend Damon gives my partner and me a historical tour of the city. Some of the houses remind my partner of England, where he is from.

I see a fox in Polly's yard.

My partner and I settle into a routine: I go to the assisted living community in the morning, we meet up at midday to do something, we spend the afternoon together at the assisted living community with my mom, and we leave in the evening.

## 16 April

When I arrive, my mom is eating breakfast. She tells me her shadow box is part of a surveillance system. *"They think I'm asleep, but I'm not."*

She writes me a note on a napkin and tells me to hide it in my bra. Obediently, I do so. I go into my room to read it surreptitiously. *"Please say absolutely nothing more to anyone now."*

She wants to know all about the high school reunion.

The sofa bed arrives. Its arrival is very confusing for my mom; she thinks they are trying to get her out of the suite. It's hard to explain that the sofa bed was ordered so that families can stay in the adjacent room.

*Sofa bed*

(My stuff is on the table, including the hospice booklet, *Gone From My Sight*.)

I take my partner for a walk in Bryan Park to see the azaleas. I'm not ready to take him on a walk in the ravine.

The next day, I arrive early to the assisted living community. My mom is still sleeping. The med tech tells me she did not wake up to take her 9 p.m. medication but slept through the night. That means she slept a lot. I let her continue. A little while later, I hear her and go into her room. "Good morning, sunshine!" I say. She surprises me by breaking into a little song I have never heard before about sunshine and flowers in May. She eats some apple sauce and a muffin and drinks some coffee. *"Can I go back to sleep now?"* she asks and promptly does. At 9 a.m. she wakes up again, *"Is there any breakfast?"* She accepts the morning medication and falls back to sleep.

I take my partner to the Virginia Museum of Fine Arts. I feel like I finally understand Pop Art and Abstract Expressionism. I like the German Expressionists. We both enjoy the India section. We eat lunch overlooking the sculpture garden, like I did with my mom last May.

At 5:30 p.m., my mom wakes up and eats her egg salad sandwich and potato chips, half of a banana, and a blackberry.

She talks to her husband on speakerphone. He tries to help her understand that the medications will not extend her life, they will just make her more comfortable while she's dying.

She finally notices and appreciates the wisteria, which earlier took the form of wintry vines.

She falls back to sleep.

At 7 p.m., I watch her firmly close her mouth against the evening medication.

## 19 April

When I arrive in the morning, she is red-skinned and mean-eyed. She looks like she is in pain. I tell her I love her, which calms her a bit. The med tech is in the hall, crushing her medication. *"Can't you just give me a pain envelope?"* she asks me. When the med tech comes in, she doesn't have the energy to sit up. *"Can you just pour it over me?"*

The hospice aide arrives. *"I don't want a bath. I just want to die."*

"Don't you want to be clean to meet your maker?" I hear the hospice aide respond.

My mom agrees. She receives a sponge bath in bed. She seems to enjoy it. She doesn't open her eyes and falls back to sleep again when it is over.

She doesn't eat breakfast.

She doesn't eat lunch.

At 5 p.m., she is too weak to get into her wheelchair to be taken to the bathroom. She uses the commode chair for the first time. She wipes herself.

She takes her wedding ring off her finger for me to give to her husband.

She doesn't eat dinner.

The assisted living community hosts a garden party for residents and their families. There is live music: banjo and stand-up bass. My partner and I attend. The music is very good. When I tell my mom about it, she complains that no one invited her. She eats some raspberry sorbet that I saved for her from the garden party.

She has a difficult time sipping through a straw. The hospice nurse agrees that it's a good idea for me to sleep at the assisted living community tonight.

My mom rubs my head. *"I'm never gonna want to go. You know that by now."* She says she wants to go back to her house and live her life.

I try out the sofa bed.

*Bluegrass Bench*

My partner and I sit on this bench to listen
to the music at the garden party.

At 5 a.m., my mom calls my name. *"I'm hungry."* She eats half of a peanut butter and jelly sandwich and sips some peach juice. She sits on the commode chair to pee. At 6 a.m., she has her Tylenol and falls back to sleep. At 8 a.m., she has half of a banana; I have the other half. She falls back to sleep again. She wakes up for her morning medication. She eats half of a piece of French toast.

She sees a squirrel at the feeder. *"She's a good mother."*

Joy comes to visit and says there are angels in the room.

The hospice social worker visits. *"I am happy and at peace and want to thank everyone."* My mom tells her, then sleeps through the rest of the visit.

She eats tiny amounts of lunch.

My partner and I take a walk in the nearby woods.

In the afternoon, she complains of pain when standing up to sit on the commode chair. She hasn't urinated since 5 a.m. The hospice nurse says maybe her kidneys are shutting down.

An hour before it's due, she asks if the med tech can bring her medication. This is the second time she has been in pain between doses. The med tech wonders again about morphine. Then my mom goes back to sleep, smiling.

Tonight, I will stay at Polly's.

In the morning, I find my mom sitting in her wheelchair with her eyes closed. When she notices me, she begins to cry. *"I'll never be safe anywhere."* I teach her a meditation about feeling safe and at home inside oneself, that deep self where we are all One. It helps calm her.

I help her into bed and feed her a piece of strawberry and some raspberry sorbet. She enjoys them.

The caregiver says my mom wanted to stay in her wheelchair for breakfast. She says my mom wondered aloud why they are still bothering with her.

The med tech and the caregivers don't understand why I am no longer allowed to spend the night. They say I am what my mom has needed all along.

The hospice nurse comes, and we change the oxycodone prescription to four times a day. The hospice nurse thinks my mom has a month now, but says her case is so surprising it could be longer.

My mom is taking an imaginary inventory of straight pins and wants us to get rid of all of them.

Polly's children and grandchildren are coming to stay at her house. My best friend from high school invites my partner and me to stay with her.

## 22 April

Earth Day

    I drive to the assisted living community early.

    My mom's door is closed.

    When I open it, she is wide-eyed. *"I'm not dead! I thought they shut the door because I was dead."* She eats all of her cornbread and some cake with milk, then asks me for a banana.

    The mail arrives. There is a letter from her cousin containing some sheet music and a note that says, "Here is your favorite song."

    "Can you sing it to me?"

    "I don't know it," I answer, "but I can read you the words."

    I start with the title *"God will take care of you,"* and to my surprise, my mom carries on with the tune and verse:

    *"Be not dismayed whate'er betide*
*God will take care of you.*
*Beneath his wings of love abide,*
*God will take care of you."*

    *"I thought maybe I'd die on Earth Day,"* she says.

My partner and I take a walk on Seminary Avenue and have corn grits and crispy Brussels sprouts for lunch at a restaurant on River Road.

    Back at the assisted living community, my mom eats some carrots, potato with sour cream, and a brownie with milk.

    She manages to get into her wheelchair to go to the bathroom, foregoing the commode chair, then wants to continue sitting in her wheelchair and not get back in bed.

*Meditating?*

## 23 April

In Catalunya, where I live, they are celebrating Sant Jordi. Everyone is gifting each other books and roses.

I arrive at the assisted living community at 10 a.m., and my mom is sitting in her wheelchair, looking like a zombie. I comb her hair and help her back into bed. She doesn't seem to know it's me.

My partner arrives with my best friend from high school; my mom gives her a smile and sings a song about bluebirds.

The pain medication four times a day seems to be helping. She is stronger when standing up.

She eats some crispy bacon.

The hospice nurse visits.

My mom enjoys having her head stroked.

## 25 April

I drop my partner off at the Virginia Museum of Fine Arts on my way to the assisted living community.

My mom tries to stand up, but she keeps sliding off the bed and I am not able to lift her back onto it. She wants to get into the wheelchair and go pee. *"Can I just pee on the floor?"* she asks when she is half off of the bed.

"Yes," I reply, "but I can't let you fall."

*"Let me go!"* she insists.

"I'm happy to let you go," I tell her, but I can't let you fall and break your hip! Then you'll really be in trouble."

She has incredible arm strength to resist me but won't put it into her legs. Can't? Finally, I help her to lie down on the floor with pillows under her head while I go find the caregivers. Two come and it takes the three of us to drag her up onto the bed again. *"I hurt!"* She shouts.

I meet my partner at the Virginia Museum of Fine Arts. We go to the cafe for lunch. I see the painting *Closed Window* by Henri Matisse and decide Raoul Dufy thinks like me.

In the afternoon, my partner holds the commode chair while I help my mom stand and pivot, but we can't get her pull-on brief back on her. *"I love you, too,"* she tells my partner. The caregiver puts a tape-on diaper on my mom instead of a pull-on brief. She screams. She is afraid she will fall off the bed. I tell my partner it will get harder from here on in.

"More committed," he says. This is his last night in Richmond. Tomorrow, he flies back home to Spain.

She eats her leftover pancake from breakfast, with some milk.

As we are leaving for the evening, my mom makes a surreal philosophical speech.

"You can plant carrots. When I was little, they taught us to plant them at school. You can put them on the windowsill with their little green tops. Watch them grow. They grow just about anywhere. The schools thought it was important to teach children how things grow. Mankind needs food, and what better way than to teach how to grow it?" Silence. "Maybe that's why cancer is so interesting. That's why they like cancer. You can watch it grow. It just grows on its own." Silence. "My mother was worried about water. Water for the world. Who will have it, who won't? There's water everywhere."

We go back to my best friend from high school's house.

I am exhausted.

## 26 April

I am exhausted.

When I arrive at the assisted living community, my mom is sitting up in bed finishing her breakfast. She eats ALL of her breakfast, plus some cake, and Girl Scout thin mint cookies.

I don't know if she peed during the night, and now I am afraid to take her to the bathroom.

The hospice aide gives her a sponge bath in bed and helps her pee while sitting on the commode chair.

*"I want to listen to jazz on the radio."*

At 4 p.m., I tell the hospice nurse my mom hasn't urinated in twenty-three hours. She texts me. "I'll grab a Foley kit I keep in my car for just INCASE."

"What's a Foley kit?" I text back.

"A Foley catheter," she answers.

I accompany my partner to the airport and return to the assisted living community to sleep.

*"I guess people become part of a story when they're gone,"* my mom says at 2 a.m.

I guess she'll make it until May. May seems like a good month to die.

The blackberry bushes have flowers now.

My mom is sleeping and snoring.

My stepsister visits with the news that her daughter is pregnant. My stepsister is overjoyed by the thought of being a grandmother. My mom hears the news and smiles and laughs.

She sleeps and snores again.

*"I love you,"* she tells my brother on speakerphone.

*"Do you love me?"* She asks me.

When I say "Yes," she replies, *"It's good for you to love me."*

She wants to eat something she can't remember the name of.

She sees and names a cowbird at the feeder.

*Brown Thrush*

I saw the brown thrush
the eastern towhee bird and
blackberry flowers.
(haiku)

*Dogwood Blossoms*

I show her my dogwood blossoms painting. *"It's well done."* I had no idea the green buds of this bush on the quarter-mile walk would be dogwood.

"Is there anything you need?" I ask.

*"No. And I want you to get out of the way."*

"Okay," I say. "I'll go put on my toe-socks."

She laughs.

The hospice nurse comes with a shadowing employee and together, they help my mom sit on the commode chair to pee. It's the first time she has urinated in thirty-six hours. I comb her matted hair. She is clinging to her spoon.

She wakes up and eats her eggs from breakfast, a bit of rice, ice cream, and Hawaiian bread.

A friend of hers arrives, and my mom is able to say *"Hi,"* smile, and tell her she loves her.

It is a very rainy day.

My mom seems more settled when I stay more hours.

It's the next to last day of April.

"*People like rhymes,*" she says. *"A rhyme a dime; I don't know why."*

We see two blue jays at the feeder.

I find the caregivers, and they help my mom up to pee for the first time in twenty-three hours. She is now what they call "a two-person assist." I figure the best help I can give her now is to make sure they get her up to pee.

I visit her husband and give him the wedding ring.

## 30 April

My mom left her house three months ago.

A man born in Germany moves into the room across the hall. My mom and I met him in the corridor a couple of weeks ago when he was visiting the assisted living community with his family to decide if he wanted to become a resident here. He was asking if anyone spoke German. He said he heard the first shot of World War II. My mom told him she spoke a little German. *"My father translated for prisoners of war after World War II."* I had no idea. I learned in 2018 that as a child, my grandfather spoke German at home. My grandfather's family came to the United States from Marburg, Germany, in 1846. My grandfather was born in 1913. I tell my mom that Hans has moved in. She remembers meeting him but is no longer interested in having conversations.

Polly comes to visit. My mom smiles when Polly tells her about the birth of her grandson.

The caregivers manage to get my mom to the bathroom. For the first time in at least five days, she poops and also pees. On the toilet, she says, *"This is a tea party. My daughter has invited everyone."* I comb her hair. New sheets are put on her bed.

The med tech says my mom is "playing possum."

## 1 May

*"Is that Karen?"* my mom asks when I walk into the room the next morning. Somehow, that question makes it all worth it. She has eaten the rice pudding and chocolate cream pie that was on her tray. *"I guess I pooped on everyone's party."*

My best friend from high school muses about the time I spent alone with my mom when I was little, and the time I am spending with her now being like bookends.

I take a walk by the river with Polly.

*"Did you say ethical or Ethel?"* I hear my mom muttering.

## 2 May

I tune into K-Love, a Christian radio station. "God's timing is perfect," the announcer says as I pull into the assisted living community parking lot.

My mom asks after Polly's grandson.

I tell my mom I love her. *"I love you too, daughter. Greatly."* She begins to cry.

*"Do people ever scream in pain?"* she asks again. After another wacky trip to the bathroom, the caregivers wonder if she is anxious. I remember the hospice nurse suggested she could have morphine before being taken to the bathroom. I ask the hospice nurse about a bedpan; she doesn't recommend those because they can be painful and cause skin breakdown.

My mom's husband and Joy come to visit. It goes well.

I take the quarter-mile walk. My mom waves to me from her window while I am filling the bird feeder with new seeds.

On speakerphone, she talks to my son and then to my brother.

She has her fingernails clipped.

*"I guess people have to decide whether to have small or large lives. Maybe you'll get tired of this adult daughter journey and go back to Europe to do whatever you do."*

"I wonder what it's like on the Other Side," I say.

*"I think half the time we're on the Other Side."*

"What do you mean?" I ask.

*"I think a lot of the time here I'm on the Other Side and not at my house."*

The med tech tells the hospice nurse that my mom did not get her pain medication last night.

## 3 May

On my way to the assisted living community, I see a deer get hit by a pick-up truck. Its body flies through the air, across four lanes, and lands on the other side of the road. I chant the Hindu "Om Tryambakam" mantra for the peaceful transition of its soul.

My mom is sleeping and snoring, evidence that last night she received the pain medication.

She has oatmeal for breakfast and is taken to the bathroom. She pees and poops. While being lifted onto the bed she bangs her shin and cries and moans. It didn't seem like much of a bang, but the skin is slightly broken, and a bruise forms quickly.

On the quarter-mile walk, I see a pair of bluebirds flying to and from their nest.

Polly visits. *"You and my daughter have another thirty-five years to be friends,"* my mom tells her.

## 4 May

Her blood pressure is 113/67. Her oxygen rate is 93. The hospice nurse and I see a rabbit and a squirrel just under my mom's window. My mom is mostly sleeping.

She wakes up, eats two raspberries, and drinks some peach juice. *"I still love you. I will always love you."*

## 5 May

I take a walk in the nearby woods.

My stepsister visits. "Do you know Jesus is your savior?" she asks my mom.

My mom calls me in. *"Karen,"* I feed her oatmeal. *"As long as you are here…"* silence.

"As long as I am here, what?"

*"As long as you are here, it will be easier, I think. You will remember the honor, the respect."*

Today Prince Charles becomes King Charles. He has a long purple train. It's a new reign.

I suspect my mom skipped her nighttime medication; she looks a bit mean-eyed. She eats some oatmeal and a banana.

I drive downtown to the Richmond Public Library. A friend who recently moved back to Spain told me her friend, a poet, is giving a reading there. My mom is an alumna of the university where this poet now teaches. After the reading, I walk down Broad Street, starting where Miller & Rhoads used to be, down to Adams Street, where there is now a statue of Maggie Walker.

*"You always want to touch everything,"* my mom tells me when I get back to the assisted living community. *"Take yourself away until tomorrow."*

I may as well obey; I need the rest.

## 7 May

The med tech tells me my mom is "loopy". She's sleeping when I arrive. There's a different smell in the room. Her hands are cooler.

A friend drives me to the garden store. The cars on both sides of the four-lane motorway stop while a mother duck crosses, ducklings in line behind her.

*"Let's have a peaceful day,"* my mom says.

She's alert the next morning. She recognizes me and smiles. *"I think you found your partner,"* and smiles again.

The caregivers help her sit on the commode chair to pee; it's been forty-eight hours.

She coughs like she's trying to cough something up.

*"Is there any milk?"* she asks, then drinks a bit of milk and eats eight spoons of yogurt.

I find the local telephone number of one of my mom's college roommates in a pile of notes my mom made while she was still at the nursing home. I call to let her know. She comes to visit and then tells me she and my mom enjoyed talking, as they always have.

*Winter to Spring.*
Loblolly pines on the quarter-mile walk.

## 9 May

Three months have passed since my mom moved to the assisted living community.

"*I want my daughter,*" she says when I come in the morning.

"I'm here," I answer.

*"I've been doing some research for your partner and I'm glad you are home with your son again."* There is a container of rice pudding in her hands; she must have opened it and tried to drink it. I feed her most of it.

"*It's best I know nothing about anything.*"

"OK," I say, "I won't tell you that I'm taking your husband to the dentist today."

"*Yeah, I don't need to know.*"

I open my mom's window and leave to take the quarter-mile walk. When I get to her window, I go close and say, "Mom? Can you hear me? I'm at the window." She turns toward the window and opens her eyes. She sees me and smiles. She is still smiling when I get back to the room.

Her roommate from college stays with her while I take her husband to the dentist.

When I get back, the roommate is still there. The caregiver is feeding my mom a peanut butter and jelly sandwich. *"Karen's not patient,"* my mom tells her college friend, *"but she tries to be."*

## 10 May

Today is Mother's Day in Mexico.

I open the curtains of my mom's window as I do every morning. *"Pray,"* my mom says.

"Always," replies the med tech, "pray without ceasing."

The hospice nurse and hospice aide help my mom to the commode chair. She poops, but no pee. The hospice nurse says my mom is "noodly," and it is unsafe to get her up anymore. The hospice nurse will insert the catheter. She palpates a hard place under my mom's ribs which she thinks may be the spread of cancer.

*"My slipper fell off,"* my mom says, while they are getting her back in bed.

In the afternoon, a friend of my mom's, whom I loved in childhood, comes to visit. She hasn't seen my mother for years. She has a son the same age as my brother. She and my mom organized the elementary school library according to the Dewey Decimal System. She brings some tulips in a pot. "You've done a great job," she tells my mom. "You did a good job as a mom; we all worry about this. You did a five-star job." She blesses my mom and tells her there are angels all around. She and I cry. It's the best day.

I change my ticket home to July 3rd. The next "potent" date is my mom's birthday, June 30th. It's hard to imagine she will still be here then. I don't want to spend the Fourth of July in the United States.

My mom tells me three times to tell my brother she loves him.

The next morning, I assure her I told my brother that she loves him. *"I know everybody loves each other,"* she replies, *"finish the work in your department."*

*"Will you stick around?"* she asks. I say yes and remind her that I am not allowed to stay at night.

I notice her morning medication has been left on the counter, and I give it to her. With the hospice nurse, we decide not to renew the multi-vitamin prescription.

On speakerphone, she talks to her husband, then my brother, then my son.

*"Where are you going next with Polly?"* She asks me.

She eats some apple slices.

I take the longer walk around the neighborhood and draw the fire hydrant with pink flowers around it.

When I come back, she finishes her peanut butter and jelly sandwich, soaked in some milk.

*Fire Hydrant*

## 12 May

The hospice nurse inserts the catheter. My mom is given liquid morphine to help with the process. Her tape-on diaper and the chuck pad underneath get soaked, plus a towel underneath and the bottom sheet, AND she releases 800 ml of urine into the catheter bag. She has been holding it for a long time.

## 13 May

The catheter seems to be a relief. She eats an entire bowl of oatmeal, then applesauce, and sweet potato pie. She drinks a glass of milk.

My stepsister visits and brings a Mother's Day card. My mom starts talking about buttons. She mutters about *"the button ride."*

*"I haven't petted the cat lately,"* she tells us.

My sister-in-law sends tulips.

There is heavy rain, with thunder and lightning.

"What do you want to do for Christmas?" my best friend from high school asks me in the evening when I tell her how much my mom ate.

It's Mother's Day.

I arrive at 7:30 a.m. It's quiet all around the place, and my mom is sleepy. "Come on, Mom, open your eyes for the Mother's Day photo," I say. She struggles to lift her eyes, then smiles for the selfie.

The med tech takes her vitals: her blood pressure is 118/60, her oxygen level is 94.

I take the quarter-mile walk and go just off the path to the gazebo. I sit on the bench, realizing that, other than the toilet, this is the last place my mom sat outside of her wheelchair.

The catheter bag is changed, and she eats half of a pot of yogurt and a raspberry.

In the afternoon, she eats most of a bowl of cream of wheat.

*Tulips are perfect for Mother's Day.*

I show her the *"Tulips are perfect for Mother's Day"* painting and put some lotion on her arms and hands. *"I wonder where that ring from my finger is,"* she says.

*The magnolias are beginning to bloom.*

## 15 May

When I arrive at 8 a.m., my mom tells me she's been waiting an hour for the med tech. Does this mean she has more pain? I wonder. I move her body a bit more to the center of the bed. She eats some ambrosia and drinks a chocolate milkshake. She thanks me for being here, and for my love.

She asks for *"Braveheart"* the eye pillow.

*"I'm so glad you could come back."*

I have to remind myself of the evidence: she has a catheter, she doesn't feed herself, and she doesn't get out of bed. Her decline is real.

*"Thank you for returning. All the uncles and aunts, goodbye."*

She thinks the med tech is me and says, *"Thank you for taking care of me, your partner, and your son."* Her vital statistics are okay this morning: oxygen 96 and blood pressure 113 over 70.

For the first time, she poops on herself. *"That's because of feeding me,"* she accuses me. She tells me and my stepsister that she is going to stop eating. She suggests I eat her share of the food.

A caregiver comes and changes her. She says there is the beginning of some skin breakdown and turns my mom onto her side. I comb my mom's hair and cut it a bit.

*"It's fascinating,"* my mom declares.

While my stepsister and I are visiting my mom's husband, my mom poops on herself again. The caregiver turns her onto her other side. When I return to the assisted living community, my mom looks small and defeated. I hold her head, and she looks up. She likes it.

## 16 May

She really wants to know now how she can get out of this.

I explain to her about the pressure sores. Her mind seems to be right here.

She still looks small. *"Thank you for making things look pretty,"* she tells me. *"Are you eating my share of the food?"*

*"I gotta get dressed,"* she says, *"You can be my little agent."*

She decides to eat her peanut butter and jelly sandwich. "Back in the game!" I say.

*"It's not a game. It's life itself."*

*"I'll retreat,"* she says, *"It will happen in its own time when I establish myself."* I give her a kiss, and she gives me one.

"I'll be back tomorrow," I say, and kiss my mom on the forehead.

When I am leaving for the night, I always give her a kiss on the forehead and say, "I'll be back tomorrow." I never say, "See you tomorrow."

## 17 May

This morning, I come in and find her squinting at something imaginary. *"It would be easier if I could see the date of the death."*

When I ask if that is possible, she is convinced it can be looked up in the records. *"Is it the 28th? the 29th?"* It's almost like she's looking at something and having a hard time making out the numbers.

I think she remembers my ticket back was yesterday as she asks, *"When did you get back?"* When I remind her that I always leave at night and come back in the morning, she says, *"Tell me about your trip."* I think she believes I went to Spain and came back. I don't tell her the date of my new ticket; I say I will stay as long as she does.

I take the quarter-mile walk around the assisted living community and talk to her through the screen of her window. She waves her pinky finger at me without opening her eyes.

I go out for lunch.

In the afternoon, she eats some strawberry mousse and a bit of oatmeal.

"What did your mom die of?"
　"My mom didn't die yet. What did your mom die of?"
　*"I don't remember."*
　"She died of breast cancer in 1981."
　*"I'm impressed."*

*End of Life Bouquet.*

There are just two weeks left in May. Then we will be in June.

## 18 May

It seems like someone fed her oatmeal during the night.

Her blood pressure is 104/66. Her oxygen level is 95.

"She is completely incontinent now," the hospice nurse tells me.

My best friend from high school comes to visit. We tell my mom we will go on the Bellevue Garden Walk this Sunday. Last year they went together.

My mom starts speaking in German. *"Ja,"* she answers and mutters something about *"Ich bin…"*

When I tell her I am leaving for the night she says, *"You haven't finished yet."* Then, *"Pray. I'm anointing every item."*

## 19 May

I have been at the assisted living community for eighty days running.

My mom enjoys eating some applesauce.

The caregiver comes to change my mom. *"I love my daughter,"* my mom tells the caregiver. *"I love my girl. I don't have a boy yet. She has my heart."* I tell the caregiver how she was alone with me. *"Keep the secrets! Don't tell the secrets!"* my mom exclaims.

"The secrets are over," I say.

*"Yay."* My mom replies.

I was in Richmond this time last year.

*A chipmunk appears at the feeder! It stuffs its cheeks with seeds!*

## 20 May

"Oh good. Let's get up and go to the bathroom," she says when I walk in.

A little while later, I am shocked to find her feeding herself apple sauce with a spoon.

I call the caregivers to change her. The entire event is quite intense, with lots of turning of her body, wiping up, sheet changing, and holding her steady so she is not afraid of falling off the bed. *"I feel like a Queen Bee,"* she says. Then suddenly, *"Do you know, Kirana, that you are my reassurance?"*

*"Can you turn off this radio?"* she asks. There is no radio. Is there noise in her head? She thanks me for turning it off.

Today I feel like I need to get out.

My mom goes from humming to snoring.

*"Eventually you and Polly will go away and do something,"* she says when she wakes up.

I walk the perimeter of the nearby woods.

I see a rabbit hopping along the path my mom sees from her window.

I sleep in the assisted living community. Throughout the night, my mom mutters and snores. At 5:30 a.m., the med tech tells me my mom has been less responsive since I stopped staying here. The hospice nurse says that's not due to my presence; it's my mom's physical process.

In the morning, I hear her from my sofa bedroom, *"I am Virginia Carpenter. I am usually right here, in this room, in this bed."*

The fun news is that the chipmunk came back to the feeder.

My best friend from high school and I go on the Bellevue Garden Walk.

When I return, my mom is muttering and has thrown off her blankets. I take the quarter-mile walk and talk to her through her window. She opens her eyes. *"I see you."*

"You be careful," I say when I leave at 7 p.m.

*"I will,"* she says, *"I won't even go anywhere."*

## 22 May

*"I need you to stay all day,"* she says when I arrive in the morning. Her sheets and blankets are in disarray.

She talks and talks and talks. She never stops muttering to herself. She's been eating an entire bowl of oatmeal, cream of wheat or grits, plus yogurt or apple sauce, every morning for the last five days, and then not much else. Today, she finishes a bowl of oatmeal, proclaims my stepsister's chocolate cherry cake *"excellent,"* drinks chocolate milk, and eats a bit of banana. She returns to her non-stop muttering.

I've been formulating the theory that since getting past the hurdle of defecating on herself, she has decided it is okay to be spoon-fed and cleaned up. This theory gains traction when I hear her tell the hospice aide, *"I'm not ready to die. I'll just lie here."*

She has been speaking in rhyme. *"I sigh, I lie, I die. They cry, we fly."*

*"We just be. We happy, lee lee lee,"* she chants while getting changed and cleaned. *"If I lie, I not bury."*

She is drifting in and out of her delirium.

*"Can you wrap me up and put me in a container with a lid where I won't hear this radio?"*

*"Can you keep all these things together and also apart?"*

*"I thank you for wrapping me up totally. Separate from anything that has stuff and radio."*

*"I need to write,"* she says and asks for a pencil. I put a pad on her lap and with her eyes closed and using the back end of the pen, her hand makes writing motions on the bedsheets while she says out loud, *"I write. Maybe come the night, but I alright."*

*"You are my pen,"* she tells me.

Polly invites me to stay the night with her. Her husband is traveling. I have a wonderful swim in the lake. I lie on the deck in the sun. I take a long, hot shower

*"Where's that other girl who stays in the next room?"* I overhear her asking the med tech. *"Katherine? Kate?"*

*"I missed you yesterday,"* she says when I go to her room and feed her cream of wheat.

*"I was here yesterday,"* I remind her, *"just not last night."*

I take a walk in the nearby woods. I see chickadees, bluebirds, and a small woodpecker.

My stepsister visits and tells my mom she loves her. She is sitting in the chair at the end of the bed. I am sitting beside my mom and hear her say quietly, *"I love my daughter. I love my son. I love you all, and now it's done."*

The chipmunks appear at the bird feeder and finish all the bird seed.

She wants someone to hold her, so I climb into bed with her for a little while.

This is the last week of May.

Tina Turner has died. She was a remarkably strong and resilient person.

When I arrive, my mom is sleeping, mostly soundly, no muttering. At 9 a.m., the muttering begins, so I go into her room. She is awake. She eats all of her oatmeal, some yogurt, and some apple sauce.

I feel like she is clinging now due to her own self-clinging. She is not here for anyone else and is not letting go, just her own clinging on to every little thing. I feel like I am being mean for thinking this. "Clinging to life is self-sustaining and exists even in the wise," says *The Yoga Sutras of Patanjali*.

She is definitely speaking in rhyme.

I am emotionally exhausted.

I realize that if I am going to continue to do this, I need to take a break. Because the yoga center I direct in Spain is affiliated with Yogaville, I can be their guest for a week. It is only a one-and-a-half-hour drive from Richmond.

*"There's a lot going on in my head,"* she tells me at 7:30 a.m. the next morning. *"Kar? I love you. We've got each other."*

I take the quarter-mile walk. She sees me outside of her window. When I return to the room, I lift her head, and she sees the chipmunk!

## 26 May

The oxycodone prescription has not arrived. My mom is alert and delirious.

I tell her I may go to Yogaville. *"You have a lot of travel bug in you."*

*"These ladies ought to show you how to collapse all the boxes so they fit in a small space."*

"Where's your son?"

"He's in Spain."

"Where's your partner?"

"He's in Spain."

*"He sure goes back and forth a lot."*

*"There's a lineup of cats and old ladies in fancy clothes."*

"Do the kids get Google boxes with colors?"

*"Do you have a June calendar I can look at?"*

*"Me and Braveheart have a dark relationship."*

"When are you going back to anywhere you go?"

"Soon."

*"You got any clothes that you call magenta that are mine?"*

She accepts a sip of coffee.

She decides to describe all the things on the shelf that she can see from her bed. *"So I'm gonna recite: there's a clock. And something Chinese that reminds me of Buddha, and a cloud that reminds me of Buddha, and the butterfly pillow, and a six- or seven-edged star* (a lily) *and a little bitty cat on the right, then magnolia flowers* (the tulips), *little ships* (some geese hand-painted on a greeting card). *"They're all fine,"* she decides. *"I don't have to do anything with them, and they can talk to each other."*

*"Sometimes I look at things and, some unwind. Some go left and some go right."*

"You think you ever want some children?"
"I have one."
"Who's she?"
"A boy, named Noah."
"Oh, of course. Excuse me for being confused. It's like you just met a stranger."
"I wonder who's talking on a radio now." (She is still hearing the radio in her head.)
She sees my journal. "That's my little dictionary, isn't it?"
She is still speaking in rhyme.
Her blood pressure is 90/60.

I go to the Virginia Museum of Fine Arts. I look at the Japanese woodblock prints.

*Squirreling Around or The Gang's All Here.*

I am trying to calm myself while she is in her delirium, so I just duplicate and triplicate all of the squirrels and robins and cowbirds I see from her window while I am sitting beside her, listening.

My mom was sleepy when I left last night, and the bowl of oatmeal and the Ensure have not been touched. She hasn't eaten in twenty-four hours.

"*Can you walk?*" she asks me when she wakes up. She talks about bells ringing and about my plans. "*Are we taking care of the things downstairs? Is there a pattern?*"

"*Is there a package to send to California? Is it ready?*"

"*Did my husband's ex-wife have a burial service?*"

"*There are times when I would get up and I would get out of this bed, and I would walk. To be in that treasury seat. Without anything being pushed, and I'm gonna eat while I'm situated.*"

"*There seem to be three or more couples at an impasse that seem to be affiliated with honey and with each other.*"

"*Has anyone brought us any kind of Bellevue supper menu that we're supposed to look at?*"

"*Would you like to have a chipmunk creature all gathered together in one place? Would it offend you if you had six or eight gathered together in one little place?*"

"*Can you give me any idea if the three people standing there by the jar of honey are still there?*"

"*Well, I eighty-four, that my private door.*"

"*That book called Master Clock - are you there?*"

"*I've been trying weeks to die.*"

Henry Kissinger, U.S. secretary of state from 1969 to 1977, turns one hundred. He is still opining about geopolitics and domestic and foreign affairs.

She asks again for a pen to write with. I give her one and open to a blank page in my journal. I don't think she will do anything, but she puts pen to paper saying, *"Take away this piece of paper. We not knowing this, we caper."*

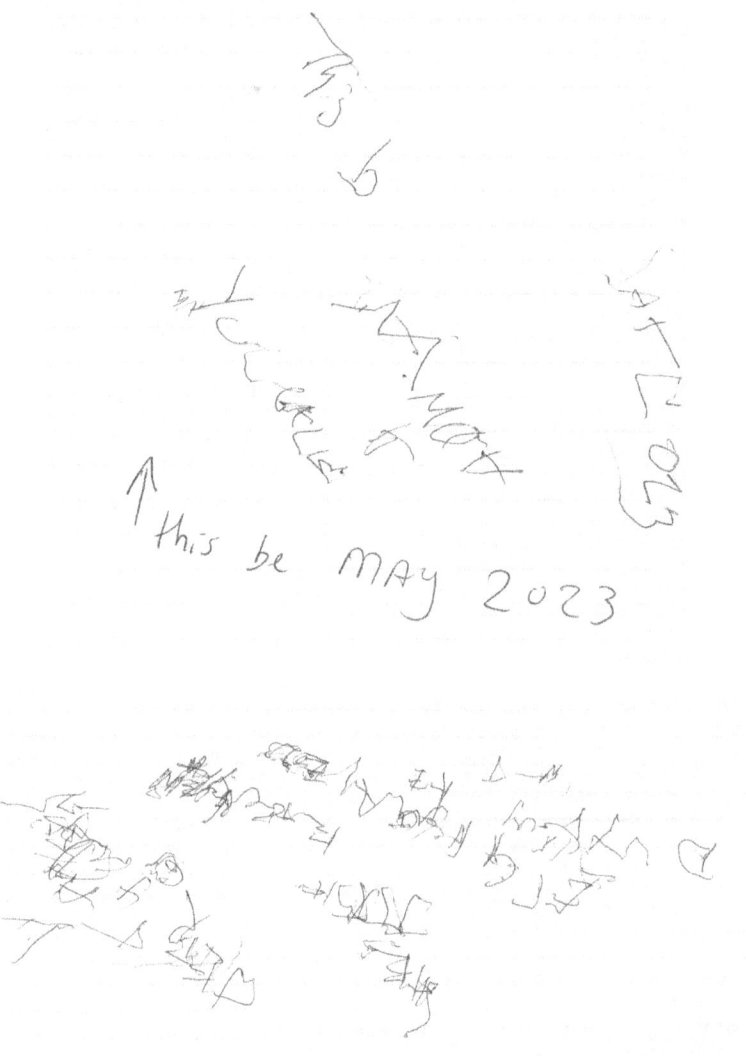

*"This be May."*

*"You two are a combination,"* she says, while the caregiver and I are changing her. Then, *"You two are lethal."* We are the lethal combination, we decide.

## 28 May

My mom seems to be more "normal" today. She's not rhyming.

There's a banana under her head. She must have tried to eat it during the night.

*"Did you talk to my sister?"*

"I told her you said you love her."

*"Tell her to tell her husband I love him."*

She eats half of the banana, then strawberry yogurt, Ensure from a spoon, and applesauce. She manages the bib/napkin on her own.

She reckons she can't sit up on her elbows or draw her knees to her chest, but she can wiggle her feet and use her hands.

"Do you still want to set your soul free?" I ask.

*"I hope so,"* she answers.

*"I love you little girl. I remember having a baby,"* she tells me at 11:30 a.m. while I am feeding her oatmeal.

The rest of the day is mostly sleeping, punctuated by eating pea soup and tapioca pudding.

*"Can I die lying down?"*

She thanks me for taking care of her and tells me I have to take care of myself as well.

## 29 May

Memorial Day

My mom is sleeping more soundly this morning, less or no muttering. She seems to have finished her pudding and Ensure during the night. Her room is cleaned and vacuumed; she sleeps through it. I check; she needs changing. She mostly sleeps through that as well but wakes up enough to say to the caregiver, *"Sam I am, braid, I have friend. I love you and you love me."* She falls back to sleep. I gather her sheets and quilt and take them to the laundry room.

Later she calls me in. *"I go today. You can help me go away. I had a piece planned, but it got out of hand."*

She says she needs all the help she can get, and that she is grateful. I hear her in her room saying, *"I give up."*

*"Start to slide, can you help me with the ride?"*

In German: *"Danke." "Ja."*

On social media, I follow the poet George Szirtes. Not knowing where else to turn, I send him a direct message:

"I have been with my mom in hospice for the last four months. At the end of January, she was diagnosed with metastasized breast cancer and, among other places, has three tumors in her brain. In February and March, she dropped a lot of verbs (she was an English teacher for part of her life) and began to speak a sort of Pidgin English, sometimes referring to herself in the third person, as a small child might. Then she recovered her language skills, but for the last two weeks, she has been speaking in rhyme!!! Her eyes are mostly closed. Here are some of her poems; have you ever heard of end-of-life rhyming?"

*I love my daughter*
*I love my son*
*I love you all*
*And now I'm done.*

*I'm eighty-four.*
*It's my private door.*

*I go today;*
*You can help me go away*
*I had a piece planned,*
*but it got out of hand.*

*I start to slide.*
*Can you help me with the ride?*

*Can you take away this piece of paper?*
*We not knowing this, we caper.*

He responds by way of a public post:
"RHYMING.

A social media friend sends me a message in which she tells me how her mother, who has been diagnosed with cancer that has metastasized to her brain, has started speaking in rhyme and rhythm. The rhymes are simple and appropriate to her situation, but they are extraordinarily moving.

Why? Maybe because even in old age, in a state of physical disorder, the mind continues to organize itself into delicate but coherent patterns. The patterns it clings to remain reassuring and empowering. (Look! I can control experience through words, thoughts, and feelings!)

Rhymes, I wrote in the past, are accidents waiting to happen - in that, the coincidence of sounds in a logical-seeming language structure seems to be merely that: a set of accidents. How, then, should these accidents, these arbitrary sounds, become part of something compelling, reassuring, memorable, almost magical?

Isn't language itself comprised of arbitrary sounds to which we have assigned meaning? In what way is the word, 'table' connected to the board on four legs? Only because we say so and continue saying so. Say it often enough, and the meaning slowly drains out of it and the sound stands there all but naked in its bare, forked nonsense.

So, everything falls apart but, somehow, the house holds together. The rooms have doors and windows, the hall leads to stairs that lead to another floor. The language-house remains predictable despite its arbitrary elements.

In this case, the mother's mind holds on to the world by playing with the arbitrary and fashioning it into sense, which is what human beings always try - and need - to do. In the long term, of course, these attempts fall short, fail, and the house comes tumbling down.

But the attempt to hold it together is noble, moving, and somehow, joyous."

The rhyming continues.
*"I love you*
*in my sleep.*
*That were good work.*
*You been deep."*
She says she wants some milk, but when I say, "You have to sip."
She replies, *"I can't sip, I'll just skip."*
I enjoy her brunch of eggs, hash browns, grits, coleslaw, and corn.
I text the hospice nurse. "She's still speaking in rhyme."

## 30 May

I'm feeling angry today.

My mom rambles and rambles.

I help her talk to her husband on the phone. I feed her grits. I give her water, watermelon, and a strawberry. She wonders about my son, and about my partner. She is muttering constantly.

"*Yes, is my heart the right space? Or my arms, the way I'm holding them to you? Has everything been arranged?*"

February. March. April. May.

"*If you don't wrap it up, don't consider it put away.*"

I walk into her room and find her feeding herself oatmeal with a spoon. "*I seeming to be okay,*" she says.

She has her fingernails clipped. One of them is cut too close to the cuticle, and she cries.

She remembers the Godiva chocolate balls I brought with me in February. I bought them at the JFK airport. "*I wish it were like those first days when we came.*"

## 31 May

"Good morning! Have a blessed day!" the toll plaza attendant tells me when I hand him seventy cents.

My mom is snoring with her mouth open.

The hospice aide gives her a bath, just her face and eyes and intimate parts. My mom loves it.

She starts talking about a goose, and I recall a song she sang to me as a small child. I sing.

"Go tell Aunt Rhody, go tell Aunt Rhody, go tell Aunt Rhody,
the old grey goose is dead.

She died in the mill pond, she died in the mill pond, she died in the millpond,
from standing on her head."

"I been knowing that song at least eighty years."

She says she loves *Braveheart* and would like to have some more eye pillows made. I tell her I bought it when I went to see Amma, the hugging saint.

"*Oma?*" she asks.

"No, Amma."

"*All different names for Momma.*"

"Somebody has a little area where they say a person's name, and you know they look at that area and consider it a specific pressure point."

She seems more mentally alert than on other days.

Her snoring is very loud.

I show her the turquoise blue sippy cup I bought for her at the big grocery store. She declares it worth keeping and wants to examine it.

Three squirrels and the chipmunk are outside.

She falls back to sleep.

## 1 June.

Month five.

I come in near 9 a.m. She has thrown off all her covers and pooped. The sippy cup is stuffed up the sleeve of her nightgown. The caregivers change her.

She begins to talk. *"This smile is for Karen."* Then, *"Your partner loves you. This message from him. I don't know why I convey. He know I love you. He love you, too."*

To me: *"Thank you for coming into my life."*

She is muttering a lot again today.

*"I hope I just tired. That's what I hope."*

I hear her muttering about Father's Day.

*"Anytime I have a daughter in this room, it help me. As long as you are still near. You can even be still. You and your little mirrors."*

*"Thank you to help me learn so much."*

"I wonder what you learned from me."

*"Oh, I could tell you. I could tell you lots and lots."*

*"Oh Karen, I so glad to have you with me here."*

*"If that help me die, I love you pouring the wave, the color. Oh my darling, oh, bye!"*

*"Let it be. Answers going flow by me. Day by day, let it by. Let them answers be. Thank you. Let's go by me. I'll get back to you."*

*"Pain in the bucket, that water keeps flowing by, thanks to buckets."*

*"You gotta stop? You'll be back, I know you'll hop."*

*"I waiting by,"* she says.

"Standing by?" I ask.

*"Lying by,"* she answers.

## 2 June

I get to the assisted living community at 7:30 a.m. My mom is sleeping and snoring. She wakes up for her medication and then falls back to sleep. The hospice nurse comes, and she wakes up again. Her blood pressure is 111/78.

She feeds herself grits, setting the bowl on her chest, and then she eats a chocolate eclair AND a peach.

She knows I am going to Yogaville tomorrow.

Polly brings her weeks-old grandson to meet my mom.

I take the quarter-mile walk. She waves and even smiles at me through her open window. *"Be safe!"*

My mom's husband and Joy come to visit. He strokes her head and touches her hand.

*"If I die in my sleep, call me."*

I help her talk to my brother on the phone.

I meet my best friend from high school at the Greek Festival. We eat spanakopita and baklava.

## 3 JUNE

I will leave for Yogaville this afternoon.

My mom is super alert, somewhat manic, and rhyming.

She is processing a lot with the muttering and the rhyming.

She says she will miss me while I am at Yogaville.

"You just bring so lovely balance. You probably bring it to anything. It's the way you do most anything."

"*I smell greenery,*
*in the scenery,*"

I move the helium butterfly into her room. It's free-floating now.

"*I left what I didn't know.*
*Let partition grow and grow.*"

I take the quarter-mile walk. She sees me through her window.

"Love you lots."

*Birds in the grass*

## 4 June

My guest room at Yogaville is beside the woods. I see a deer.

On my way to Sivananda Hall, where meals are served and celebrations are held, I see a baby rabbit.

No news of my mom.

*Sivananda Hall Yogaville*

The food is nourishing, light, energizing, reviving, vegetarian.

Every morning at dawn, I attend meditation and then again at noon, and 6 p.m. I attend hatha yoga classes after the morning meditation, and sometimes before the 6 p.m. meditation.

In the foothills of the Blue Ridge mountains, I sing the Nirvana Shatakam which is, in a nutshell, about not being anyone, anything, anywhere. I am nothing. I am beyond.

Everything flows.

The hospice nurse texts me. "Hi! Saw your momma today. She looks stable! Got a bed bath and had a big bowel movement. I walked in this morning, and she was sleeping with a huge smile on her face."

My stepsister tells me that when she arrived to visit my mom, the helium butterfly had floated out into the corridor of the assisted living community. She brought it back in. It floats closer to the floor now.

There is a shooting in Richmond in Monroe Park after a high school graduation. My partner and I walked there when he visited. Seven are wounded by gunfire, and by the evening, two of the wounded are dead.

The hospice chaplain visits my mom.

The caregiver sends me an email.

> Hello! I hope you are doing well and relaxing! I just wanted to let you know your mom is doing well. Yesterday, I noticed her mouth was very dry because she keeps her mouth open. I wanted to lubricate her mouth, but she was having difficulty sucking on a straw. So, I saw those sponge sticks. I dipped one into her orange juice, and she LOVED IT. It was also effective. So, I did it again this morning. Every time I go in to check on her, her eyes are closed. So, I go up to her and say, 'Good morning, beautiful.' She knows it's me from my voice and calls my name. That makes my heart melt! She asked about you this morning, she said, *'She is on a break. Yes, her break from all this…'* Your mom is aware! I've said this forever. She knows. Anyway, I just wanted to let you know she's doing okay. Rest, relax, do whatever you want/need for YOU."

*"I could have made so many different decisions during my life,"* my mom tells Polly when she visits, *"but I made the ones I made. And now it's over."*

The pujari dedicates the noon ritual of offering light, flowers, and water to the divine, to my mom.

In Sanskrit *"Jyothi Chaksusha Pasyati"* means "The light that sees through the eyes."

Someone suggests I see the painting by Artemisia Gentileschi at the Virginia Museum of Fine Arts when I get back to Richmond.

I see two foxes at dawn and a bobcat in the evening.

The caregiver sends another email. "I swear she's rhyming again today! It's very interesting. Not making sense, but the last word of every phrase rhymes! I love it."

## 10 June

The hospice nurse texts to tell me that she replaced the catheter and put my mom on antibiotics for a yeast infection. The hospice nurse is going on a two-week vacation. I will not be able to contact her. There will be a substitute hospice nurse. She assures me, "She knows all about your mom so it should be a good fit."

"Can you guess any timeline?" I ask. "I imagine you're expecting her to be here when you get back."

"No, she's a hard one to guess," the hospice nurse texts back.

If my mom needs me, I need the hospice nurse.

On my drive home, I see vultures feeding on a carcass by the roadside.

I get back to the assisted living community at sundown. My mom seems to be holding steady on her plateau.

"I'm back from Yogaville," I announce.

*"I want some yoga on a spoon,"* she replies. I feed her mashed potatoes, oatmeal, peach yogurt, and two slices of canned mandarin orange.

*"You here now,"* she says. *"It be safe around us."*

## 11 June

My mom begins to use archaic personal pronouns. The caregiver calls it biblical speech.

*"I love thee so!"* she greets me when I arrive in the morning.

*"Thee daughter. Thee know."*

Repeating themes are *"Thee go." "Ye go." "Thee task." "Thee ask." "Me go." "The picture show."*

*"Oh celery, we been telling task. Thee task, thee task."*

*"Let me ask it, let me die, that thee call me."*

I go to Polly's house and swim in the lake with all her grandchildren.

## 12 June

When I arrive at the assisted living community, my mom is sleeping, then wakes up and starts talking. *"I need help,"* she says. I open the window and rearrange her blankets. I wait for the caregivers to come and change her.

*"I always want too much cash. That's me."*

*"I know there's food, and I don't want any more. It'll be okay."*

While the caregivers are changing her, she says, *"I got nothing left. I just want to die."*

I take the quarter-mile walk. I say hello to her through her window. She opens her eyes. *"I see you,"* she says.

She eats some oatmeal. She loves sipping a bit of water and enjoys being spoon-fed some orange juice.

The hospice chaplain visits briefly.

*"I just don't do much, I guess."*

The substitute hospice nurse visits. She is kind. At the end of the visit, my mom opens her eyes to look at her.

I take the longer walk around the neighborhood. When I return, my mom is attempting to feed herself lentil soup.

The skin behind her left shoulder is speckled with red. There is more sediment in her urine.

She needs to be changed again and complains of pain while that is happening. All her sheets are changed. When offered her medication, she says, *"I think it's silly to take a pill-y"*

My son phones me. "Talk to your grandmother," I say. I want to see if she will respond.

"Mom, it's your grandson," I say. To my surprise she opens her eyes; I ask him to switch quickly to video.

*"That Noah!"* she exclaims. *"He handsome!"*

She's fidgeting with her sheets. "Can you fold a washcloth?" I ask, handing her one.

*"I don't know,"* she answers, then covers her face with it.

She eats oatmeal, vanilla yogurt, and coconut cream pie. *"You ain't got the spoon right. You got a right bright moon."*

I take the quarter-mile walk and see a hawk on the lawn. It is hopping about, and I wonder if it can fly. Then I notice it has a small songbird in its talons which it releases, then recaptures.

*"It's that beautiful Latin, that came from satin."*

In her mind, she seems to be counting and organizing socks.

## 13 June

Since I have been at the assisted living community, five residents have died.
   *"She died on my birthday as a little girl."*
   Today, the theme is *"ask, task, mask."*
   She throws off her cover, pulls up her nightgown, and *"asks"*.
   She doesn't eat anything.

## 14 June

Today is my grandparents' wedding anniversary.

My mom seems more distressed and less present today. She is happy when I hug her. She drinks water from the sippy cup better than through a straw.

She is still asking, tasking, and masking.

She eats a little bit of tapioca pudding.

*"Plant me, hope me, jackle me."*

*"I think I got a far sleeve at home."*

She manages to reach her water bottle on her own, lifting it from the bedside tray to her lips.

Her hands and feet are quite cool.

I sing the Om Shanti chant. *"Three blankets, no, two, one of them go under the Shanti. Banti Shanti, one Shanti over, Shanti under me, Shanti under that task, maybe Shanti over. Need a Shanti big."*

The med tech tells us it's going to rain. My mom finds a word that rhymes, *"brain"*, starts finding other words that rhyme, then suddenly asks, *"Karen, how's your brain?"* She opens her eyes and looks at me. She seems present. She finds more words to rhyme, *"Jane, chain…"*

## 15 June

At midnight, the month of June will be half over.

She is sleeping when I arrive, then muttering. She needs to be changed. She asks for yogurt. She enjoys a raspberry. The caregivers change her. The skin on her back is covered with red speckles.

*"I love you, Momma mask,"* she says to me, while I feed her.

A baby squirrel comes to the bird feeder. The activities director brings my mom some red carnations. My mom opens her eyes to see them. *"Beautiful."*

Jonathan the Juggler tells me he wants to perform for her again. We arrange for him to come on Saturday, two days from now.

*"Me ask. Thee ask. What me ask?"*

*Quarter-mile walk woods*

*Hello little chipmunk*

## 16 June

Unless her catheter has been changed during the night, she has had no urinary output. I caress her face and chest. *"Thank you. More than anything, it's soothing."*

She coughs. *"Let's keep askin' sump'n'."*

I take the quarter-mile walk. "I'm outside of the window, Mom. I love you," I say when I reach her window.

*"I love you, too. Now."*

She asks for water. She is expressing herself more clearly today.

"You were with me when I came in," I tell her. "I guess I'll be with you when you go out."

She smiles. *"Uh-huh."*

I hear her in her room saying, *"I just wish I were gone."* Then, a little while later, *"You want me to stay longer."*

She enjoys chicken broth and eats a little yogurt and some applesauce.

The substitute hospice nurse comes. My mom's blood pressure is 91/74. Her oxygen level is 92. She has had no urinary output. *"I love you, Karen,"* my mom says. I wonder if I should stay the night. The substitute hospice nurse will come again on Monday. I ask her if there is any reason to believe my mom's condition will change over the weekend.

"No," says the substitute hospice nurse, *"She's just chillin'."*

Polly visits. We go out to do some errands. *"Where are you two off to so fast?"*

*Good Morning Little Rabbit*

I show my mom my "Good Morning Little Rabbit" painting. *"That's beautiful. That's gonna keep me singin'. Thanks."*

I oblige my mom to open her eyes to see what I believe will be her last rainstorm.

On my way back to my best friend from high school's house, I stop off at the Virginia Museum of Fine Arts. On Wednesdays, Thursdays, and Fridays, it stays open until 9 p.m. I decide that next week, I will go those evenings on my way back from the assisted living community.

*Virginia Museum of Fine Arts Sculpture Garden.*

## 17 June

In two weeks, it will be July.

She is sleeping when I arrive. When the med tech comes in, my mom calls my name. *"Karen."* She still knows I am here. She has had no urinary output. She eats a strawberry and a bit of oatmeal.

*"I have a plan."*

Jonathan the Juggler comes. "Jonathan's here to juggle for you Mom!" I say.

Her eyes remain firmly shut. Jonathan starts talking in his professional voice, asking about my brother, about my mom's husband. Her eyes remain closed. He begins the show anyway.

"Mom," I say, "It's your last chance to see Jonathan juggling." She makes the effort to drag her eyes open and watches six or seven red balls going around in the air. She looks at Jonathan.

*"You look good. You be good,"* she tells him. *"Thank you for coming."*

Jonathan thanks her for her forty years of patronage. As Jonathan is finishing, the caregiver walks into the room to take the lunch order. My mom opens her eyes again and sees her. *"That my Sam I am. You beautiful."*

I take the quarter-mile walk and see a bluebird.

I take a walk in the nearby woods and a five-foot-long black snake crosses the path.

I tell my mom her husband misses her. *"I. Miss. My. Husband."*

## 18 June

Father's Day

In the morning, I walk to my mom's house to wish her husband a happy Father's Day before driving to the assisted living community.

My mom is sleeping when I come in. She wakes up and begins *"asking."*

*"I don't feel good at all,"* she says suddenly.

The catheter bag is empty. It looks purple.

The skin on her legs is mottled. I read online that this happens in the last week of life.

*"The pain is so brain it helps."*

"Where is the pain?"

*"I don't know. Your brother might know. Blue E. Coli. I don't know."*

*"Let me ask anything. Let me ask… thee want me pray – yes – thee ask of me let go."*

I feed her a spoonful of potato soup. *"I don't much like soup,"* she says but enjoys a few slices of canned mandarin orange.

She has a giant poop.

"Being with your mom has made me realize I want to study to be a hospice nurse," the caregiver tells me while we are changing her.

Before I leave, she is changed again. I wonder once more if I should stay the night, but there is no real reason to believe tomorrow will be any different than today.

"I'll be back tomorrow," I tell her and kiss her forehead.

I have not been in the United States since Juneteenth became a federal holiday. By searching online, I find a celebration that's on my way home.

I tell my best friend from high school I'm going to change my ticket again.

## 19 June

Juneteenth

Pulling into the assisted living community parking lot, I feel joyful. I'm excited to see my mom. There are things I want to tell her.

"Happy Juneteenth," I say to the med tech, who is in the corridor with her cart.

I walk into the suite. The door to my mom's room is closed.

"Who closed her door?" I ask out loud. "They should know she doesn't like that," I think to myself. I open the door.

"Mom?" I say.

Then "Mom."

She is still.

I take a step closer.

She is gone.

My first thought is "Wow, Mom. You did it," and I tell her so out loud.

Next, I have the strange sensation of being at a big party, from which the host has snuck out through a back door.

I take off the tape-on diaper. Her belly is still warm. I comb her hair and clean her up. I kiss her forehead.

I text her sister, my stepsister, my brother, and my partner. I phone her husband.

I hear the caregiver in the corridor and call her name. She comes in. "I just started my shift," she tells me, "I found out fifteen minutes ago."

The med tech found my mom unresponsive at 6:30 a.m.

My stepsister arrives.

The assisted living community is not allowed to call me until someone from the external hospice care comes and proclaims the death. The hospice nurse is on vacation. The substitute hospice nurse's car broke down. A different hospice nurse, who is on duty at the nearby hospital, has been called. He arrives at 8:35 a.m. and proclaims the death.

The hospice aide arrives. She was scheduled to come anyway. She bathes my mom and puts lotion on her body. I help. We change her into the blue nightgown her husband bought her for Christmas.

Someone from the funeral home arrives to take my mom's body away. We cover it with a soft woven cloth she cherished because it belonged to her mother and because it feels like down. On top of that, we place a quilt. My stepsister and I accompany the funeral home employee and my mom's body to the van that is waiting. We watch the van drive away. My mom's body will be cremated. My mom is gone from my sight.

I ask my stepsister to take the quarter-mile walk with me. When we come around to my mom's window, the baby squirrel is at the bird feeder.

"Come to my house," Polly says when she finds out. I go to her house, and we take the paddleboat out on the lake. We paddle the perimeter of the lake for two hours in the sun. "We didn't know what could happen when our moms die," says Polly as I am leaving to go back to my best friend from high school's house.

"Yeah," I say, "Now we know you might go paddle-boating on a lake."

When I arrived in February, my best friend from high school had just decided to try a dating app. After a few false starts, she has met her match. He sends us a bouquet to share, with red roses for her and white lilies to honor my mom.

*Juneteenth Flowers*

The obituary my mom wrote is published in the Sunday edition of the *Richmond Times Dispatch*.

We celebrate my mom's birthday with a memorial at "*the patio.*" I walk from my best friend from high school's house to my mom's. I turn left as I come out of my friend's house. At the bird feeder of the house two doors down, I see a house finch.

The guests come and go. Among them, family, neighbors, the neighborhood florist, my best friend from high school and her new partner, a few other friends from high school, Polly, my mom's college roommate, a yoga colleague, and the organ player from my grandfather's church.

"Your mom was the matriarch of the block," one of the local business owners tells me.

"Who's this party for?" ask some passersby.

I take a walk in the ravine and scatter some of the ashes that were my mom's body.

*Bill "Bojangles" Robinson*

My mom's favorite statue in Richmond was always Bill "Bojangles" Robinson on the corner of Adams and West Leigh Street in Jackson Ward.

I am surprised to learn it was erected on her birthday in 1973. Fifty years ago. This painting is the view from the bench below the statue.

## Afterword

In the end, I did spend the Fourth of July in the United States. The day before my mom died, I told my best friend from high school I had decided to change my ticket. I had been there so long; I needed some time to unwind from it all and integrate somehow. The next potent date was August 6th, my grandfather's birthday. I changed my flight for the fourth time.

I spent time with my friends from high school. I took walks with Joy in my childhood neighborhood. I went to Polly's lake. I took the bus downtown. I returned to the Virginia Museum of Fine Arts; I went to the Benjamin Wigfall exhibit as my mom's guest because she was still a museum member. Every Wednesday, I went to see Jonathan the Juggler at a local restaurant where he had a regular gig. I spent another week at Yogaville. I visited my mom's husband and went through things in the house. I took the train to Baltimore to see my friend, Damon, and another train from there to Philadelphia to visit The Barnes Foundation. I booked my train ticket back to Main Street Station downtown, my mom's favorite building in Richmond. When I walked out of the station, my best friend from high school and her partner were sitting on the stairs, an uncanny synchronicity. They gave me a ride back to her house.

*Philadelphia 30th St. Station*

Due to various weather incidents, my plane home landed twenty-four hours late, arriving exactly forty-nine days after my mom *"let her soul go free."* Tibetan Buddhists believe that when someone dies, there is an in-between stage known as the bardo which can take up to forty-nine days. A soul without a body, in a transient state, can better accept the law of truth, gain enlightenment, and move on to the next life.

## Acknowledgments

I'd like to thank my friend Marianne Maili, author of *Lucy, go see.* and *I am home*. She knows what it's like.

Thanks to Michael Goldfarb, author of *Emancipation: How Liberating Europe's Jews from the Ghetto Led to Revolution and Renaissance* and *Ahmad's War and Ahmad's Peace: Surviving Under Saddam, Dying in the New Iraq*, for "introducing" me to George Szirtes. Thanks to George himself for his reflection on my mom's rhyming and permission to use it in this book.

The peanut butter and jelly haiku was written by Ulrika Schygulla.

I am grateful to my friends and family in Richmond and elsewhere for providing me with support in the form of housing, transport, meals, conversations, phone calls, emails, and text messages. Thanks to all of you who took the time to read the manuscript along its way.

A special shout to Polly Stephens for opening her heart and home and telling me about The Barnes Foundation, and to Damon Silvers for getting me to Baltimore, taking me to see the Cone sisters' Matisse collection, and introducing me to Merrill Leffler.

Thanks to Helen Iles, author of *Hiraeth, Our Longing for Belonging* and editor of *Grounded, A Pandemic Anthology*, for suggesting I look for a publisher in my hometown.

From the outset E. Harpst, Robert Pruett, Liz Knapp, and the rest of the Brandylane Publishers team have made me feel like I am in the capable hands of the *No. 1 Ladies' Detective Agency*.

And, of course, thanks to my mom, without whom, none of this would have been possible.

I miss her. *Greatly.*

*Sitges Cemetery November 2023*

    It wasn't until November that I was able to decipher the words *"I paint you"* on my mom's crayon drawing of Spring.

## Postscript

In October 2017, one of our pet gerbils died suddenly. He had an operation the day before, which was supposed to end a saga spanning six months and six generations of gerbils. I found him in his cage early in the morning. My son, then thirteen, came downstairs. We were looking at Grey's little body together. I felt nauseous. From the emotional shock, I imagined. "I'm just going to see if I can get rid of this nausea by vomiting," I said to my son. Nothing came up.

"This is silly," I thought to myself, "It's just a gerbil. I'll get up and make the school snack and get on with the day." When I stood up, I took a few steps, then fainted and fell backward, banging my head on the terracotta tile floor. I didn't know that nausea can indicate low blood pressure. When I stood up, it must have dropped completely. My son heard a clunk that was my head hitting the floor. He came over to where I was lying, pulled gently at my hair, and said, "Mami?"

I came to and thought, "Well. NOW I'll get up and make the snack," but I couldn't sit up because everything was spinning.

By then, my partner had come downstairs, wondering why there was so much commotion about the gerbil. My son was asking me questions like "What is seven times eight?" I told my partner where to find the phone number for my insurance, which covers home visits. My son asked if he should go to school, and I said yes.

When the doctor came, he also asked me questions like "What is seven times eight?". He did some neurological tests with a small flashlight. My elbows hurt almost as much as my head; the doctor explained that to save our brain, the Moro reflex causes our elbows to shoot out if we fall backward unconscious.

After four hours under observation at home, the doctor sent me to the hospital by ambulance because I was still too dizzy to get up. The hospital did a CT scan and ascertained that my brain was okay. I stayed overnight. I was advised to rest for two or three weeks and then see my general practitioner. Five weeks later, I was diagnosed with a concussion.

People told me I was lucky not to be on the Other Side. Was I? "How do they know this is the lucky side?" I wondered to myself.

In late November, I booked tickets to Richmond to celebrate my mom's eightieth birthday the following June. I never imagined I would still be suffering from the head injury seven months later. I still had sensory overload. I couldn't stand for long periods or walk long distances. I couldn't walk fast or run. I realized I would be able to manage the flight if I asked for wheelchair assistance.

My son and I flew into JFK and spent a few days in Brooklyn with one of my friends from college. We visited the One World Trade Center and saw the view from the observatory. We took the subway to Central Park; I lay on the grass while my son fed squirrels and birds from his hand. My friend from Vermont came down and went with us to the Brooklyn Botanical Garden. We took a ferry from Brooklyn to Port Authority, then a Greyhound bus to Richmond.

My son and I stayed with my best friend from high school. She took me to see a neurologist at the VCU Health Center. He confirmed that I had a concussion. "You're in the 15% of what we call 'the miserable minority' who, for reasons unknown to us, take over six months to recover."

My mom celebrated her birthday at a fancy ice cream parlor. She invited some neighbors who were my son's age. Later, she and my son went to see the movie *The Incredibles*. It was a special visit, even more so in retrospect. I didn't see my mom again until the May 2022 visit.

In January 2020, I began to paint with watercolors as a sort of therapy for my head. Because I wasn't able to distract myself by watching series and films or listening to music during what I call the "Quarantime," I sheltered at home painting.

I continue painting from my present perspective.

Paradoxically, the time I spent with my mom was easier for me because of how much my head injury still slowed me down.

## ABOUT THE AUTHOR

**Kirana**, née Karen, grew up in Richmond, Virginia. Her elementary education was at Richmond Montessori, and she graduated from Open High School. She loved writing and at age thirteen won "best book" prize for a contest at the Henrico Public Library for her illustrated book *Nike* about a ten-year-old girl who meets two-inch extra-terrestrials (Nikens) that give birth to their androgynous young by blowing bubbles and lack immunity to chicken pox.

At Antioch College, she designed her own major, "World Philosophy," combining her studies of philosophy and anthropology in a senior thesis about how dreams can be used to solve conflict. After graduating, she wandered for four years in Europe, and lived on the Balearic Islands of Ibiza and Mallorca. She returned to Richmond in 1991 to become a responsible adult and be near her family. While there, she worked at an early childhood daycare center. Deciding against graduate school, she was certified as a yoga teacher. In 1993, she returned to Spain and has lived since then in Catalunya, near Barcelona. She shares a home in her "peaceful village" with her partner and young adult son and has been the director of her own yoga center since 2001.

www.ingramcontent.com/pod-product-compliance
Lightning Source LLC
Chambersburg PA
CBHW042134160426
43199CB00022B/2911